BUYING, OWNING AND SELLING A FLAT

a Consumer Publication

edited by Edith Rudinger

published by Consumers' Association
publishers of **Which?**

Which? Books are commissioned and researched by
The Association for Consumer Research
and published by Consumers' Association,
2 Marylebone Road, London NW1 4DX
and Hodder and Stoughton,
47 Bedford Square, London WC1B 3DF

© Consumers' Association Ltd August 1988

ISBN 0 340 40455 8
and   0 852 202 350 2

Photoset by Paston Press, Loddon, Norfolk
Printed and bound at the University Printing
House, Oxford

BUYING, OWNING
AND SELLING
A FLAT

a Consumer Publication

Consumers' Association
publishers of **Which?**
2 Marylebone Road
London NW1 4DX

4

CONTENTS

Foreword 7
Setting the scene 9
understanding the language, what is a lease?
Before the contract 15
preliminary enquiries, survey, local searches, gazumping
The contract 22
fixtures, exchange of contract, the deposit, completion
Arranging a mortgage 35
Summary: a typical transaction 46
Breach of contract 49
rescission, enforcing completion, compensation
The lease 54
stamp duty, guided tour of the lease, covenants, assignments,
underleases, sale of freehold
The complex chain of liability 70
effect of assignment, effect of subletting
When the professional gets it wrong 75
negligence, Defective Premises Act 1972
More about covenants 84
express obligations of landlord and of tenant, 'the usual
covenants', implied obligations
Joint ventures and misadventures 94
buying a flat together, co-ownership
The flat as the matrimonial home 100
common law right, the Matrimonial Homes Act 1983,
the ex-matrimonial home
Co-ownership by implication 104
'trust for sale', buying a flat for someone else
Service charges 114
estimates and consultation, sinking fund, tenants' association
The management and the management company 125
Enforcing the covenants 131

Fitness, repair and safety 140

Disrepair: further local authority action 153

New steps in the right direction 161
appointment of a manager, acquisition order, variation of leases, the right to information

Ending the lease 168
expiry of time, merger and surrender

When time has run out 171
protection under the Landlord and Tenant Act 1954, the Protection from Eviction Act 1977 and the Leasehold Reform Act 1967

Options and pre-emptions 177
options to renew, options to buy, rights of pre-emption, right of first refusal

When money runs out 184
charging order, bankruptcy, the Insolvency Act 1986, mortgage default

Council flats: the right to buy 193

Flats in Scotland 198
looking for a flat, making an offer, conveyancing, what you own and what you can/cannot do, repairs and maintenance, selling your flat

Glossary 226

Index 239

Throughout this book

for 'he' read 'he or she'

FOREWORD

In recent years, flat ownership has become increasingly popular. In London, and in many major cities, house prices have soared to such an extent that many people can afford only to buy the lease of a flat.

The conveyancing process is similar to that when a freehold house is bought and sold, but the relationship between landlord and tenant brings with it a variety of different considerations and added legal complications.

The landlord sells the right to occupy the flat in return for a substantial capital payment but retains many rights and obligations over the premises. The tenant buys the temporary ownership of the flat subject to a large and varied number of restrictions and liabilities.

Particular complications arise when the landlord sells the freehold and/or the tenant assigns his lease or creates a sublease out of it. In such situations, the legal position of all the parties is complex and difficult to work out.

At the root of the landlord and tenant relationship is the lease, the assignment or the sublease. Written in lawyers' language (and baffling for most people) such documents state what is being sold and detail precisely the terms and covenants upon which the transaction is based. These documents need to be studied carefully. The covenants (as the binding terms in a lease are called), in particular, need to be understood because they bind the original landlord and tenant for the duration of the lease and are transferred also to any future buyers of the landlord's and tenant's interests.

Apart from the lease, further rights and obligations affecting the landlord and tenant and their successors are to be found in many Acts of Parliament and decisions of judges.

These aspects of the law are liable to change and are difficult to keep track of.

Recent legislation includes most notably the Housing Act 1985 and the Landlord and Tenant Act 1987, which have introduced major changes in the law, which benefit the tenant. The Housing Bill 1988 (the details of which, at the time of writing, have to be finalised by Parliament) will alter the position further and, on balance, will favour the landlord. As far as is possible, the anticipated effect of this legislation as been included in this book.

Judge-made law is particularly relevant because it implies certain terms into the lease. It helps to maintain the quality of life in the flat by giving the tenant further protection against the landlord and other third parties, for example in cases of negligence and nuisance.

This book considers the rights and liabilities of the parties to a lease, but it must be remembered that to enforce them a court action, as a last resort, is necessary. This is time consuming and can prove expensive. It is much better to try to sort things out with the landord and/or other flat owners before threatening legal action. Good relations between landlord, tenant and neighbours make life a lot simpler and living in the flat much more enjoyable.

Michael Haley

Department of Law
University of Keele

SETTING THE SCENE

This book starts at the point when you have found the flat or maisonette you want to buy and are now faced with the necessary legal and administrative steps, and also some practical and financial ones.

Most of what is said about flats applies also to maisonettes. A maisonette is, generally speaking, similar to a self-contained flat with its own separate entrance, but on two floors, with no common stairs. There may be a common garden or shared water tank in the roof space.

understanding the language

Lawyers have developed a language of technical terms and expressions, often incomprehensible to the lay person. This is particularly evident when looking at leases (as dealt with later on) and the various covenants which are included in them (explained later in the book). Coming to grips with some of this language is a necessary evil, and certain key concepts need to be understood.

○ The person who creates, or grants (the words are interchangeable) a lease is known as the lessor or the landlord; the person to whom it is granted is the lessee or tenant.

○ When a lease is created, the landlord retains the freehold of the property. This is known as the landlord's 'reversion' because at the end of the lease the property reverts back to the landlord, subject to certain exceptions (which will be considered in due course). At any one time there are two owners of the property, the landlord and the tenant but each owns a different interest: one owns the freehold, the other the leasehold.

○ The landlord can sell ('assign') the freehold and the tenant can assign the remaining period of his lease. The effect of such assignments is that a new landlord or a new tenant steps into the shoes of the original parties (this can happen any number of times in the course of a lease). The original parties to the lease remain liable on the conditions (known as covenants) contained in the first lease.

○ If the tenant creates a new tenancy, for a shorter period than his lease, in favour of someone else, this is known as a sublease or underlease. The parties to the transaction are known as the sublessor and the sublessee or subtenant. With this arrangement, the original tenant, as sublessor, can exercise direct control over the flat and ensure that the conditions in the lease, for which he always remains liable, are observed by the subtenant.

EXAMPLES:

1) John leases a flat in 1970 for 99 years to Desmond. In 1988, Desmond sells the entire lease to Mary. John remains the landlord, Desmond drops out of the picture and Mary takes the assignment of the rest of the 99-year lease, which then has 81 years left to run.

2) John leases a flat in 1970 for 99 years to Desmond. Desmond creates a sublease of 25 years for Mary. John remains the landlord, Desmond is the tenant of John and the sublessor to Mary and Mary is the sublessee. At the end of 25 years, the remaining 74 years revert back to Desmond and, when this period expires, the premises revert back to John.

what is a lease?

Unlike a freehold which gives the buyer what is, for all intents and purposes, complete ownership of the land and the building(s) on it for ever, a lease confers only a limited ownership in the property, for a fixed period of time. The lease is carved out of the freehold of the landlord and can take various forms.

At one end of the spectrum there is the tenancy of a furnished bed-sit, providing short term accommodation at a weekly rent; at the other end is the long term lease bought for a large capital sum, with only a nominal rent payable.

formal aspects

For a lease, there are several conditions which must be met:

○ the parties must intend to enter into a legally binding contract;
○ the lease must be of a certain length which is either specified (for example, 99 years) or, in the case of periodic tenancies, it must be capable of being ascertained (for example, by 4 weeks' notice to quit);
○ the date when the lease starts must be stated;
○ the landlord must retain the reversion (but this may subsequently be sold);
○ the transaction must convey what is known as 'exclusive possession' which is, essentially, the right to occupy the premises to the exclusion of all others, including the landlord;
○ the agreement must be created by deed if it is for a fixed period of more than 3 years.

Leases may be either of periodic duration (weekly, monthly or yearly, for example) or for a fixed number of years (for instance, 99, 200, or 999 years). Once he has bought a long lease, the tenant's financial responsibility to the landlord is limited to a small ground rent and any service or management charge (often substantial) stipulated by the lease. It is with the long, fixed term lease that this book is concerned.

a wasting asset?

Most occupiers under a long lease will not regard themselves as tenants, but rather as owners of the property. For most purposes this is very near to the truth of the matter. The leaseholder can sell the unexpired period of the tenancy for such price as the market will bear. The lease, although declining in value with the passing of time, will for many years continue to rise in value. Indeed, for the greater part of the lease, what the tenant has can be more valuable than what the landlord has.

Below a certain number of years (40 years, for example) the lease may become less marketable, or marketable only to a cash buyer because of difficulty in getting a mortgage for a comparatively short lease. The value of the property may also be depressed by lack of maintenance and unchecked deterioration of adjacent flats. This is a cause for concern for people who live in a block of flats and can give rise to many legal difficulties which will be considered later.

why are there long leases?

There are several reasons why a long lease is granted instead of the sale of the freehold:

○ the landlord may not own the freehold of the property and, because a seller cannot sell more than he owns, a lease may be the most that can be sold;

○ the landlord may wish to derive income from the ground rent payable and may view the long term prospect of the property reverting back at the end of the lease as an inheritance to leave for future generations;

○ the landlord may wish to retain a high degree of control over the premises. Except in the simplest case (for example, a house converted into two flats), a scheme has to be worked out, which covers all the flats in the building, whereby the upkeep of the whole building is ensured. As will be shown, the lease can impose a variety of conditions (known as covenants) by which the tenant is bound. In a block of flats, for example, it is essential that covenants regulating maintenance, repair and insurance are enforceable against each flat-owner. Where one person is living on top of the other it is important for ceilings, walls, floors etc. to be kept in good repair. This would be impossible to achieve if the freehold to the individual flats were to be sold. Such covenants cannot be enforced in law between freeholders unless a contract exists between them. Buying a leasehold flat usually brings with it many obligations which would not be associated with the purchase of a freehold;

○ the general unavailability of mortgage finance for freehold flats is a practical reason for leasehold flats. Because of the unenforceability of some covenants between freeholders, building societies are reluctant to lend on freehold flats.

freehold flats

In theory it is possible to buy the freehold of a flat which is separate from the freeholds of the rest of the building. This is known as a 'flying freehold'. Building societies and other financial institutions are reluctant to lend money on flats with a flying freehold. A freehold flat is, therefore, difficult to find and mortgage finance difficult to obtain.

Other methods by which tenants may, as a group, acquire the freehold of the building are considered later in the book.

BEFORE THE CONTRACT

Having found a flat, the buyer usually enters an oral agreement with the seller to buy the property for a stated price. An oral agreement is not binding and it would be very unwise to commit such an agreement into writing. In all correspondence, the buyer and the seller should use the words "subject to contract".

The creation or transfer of a lease involves two stages: entering into a formal contract and proceeding to completion. When all the preliminary negotiations have taken place, the seller and buyer will enter a contract under which the lease of the property is to be conveyed to the buyer.

The parties usually instruct their respective solicitors or conveyancers to act for them. As a general rule, one firm of solicitors cannot act for both the seller and the buyer, so as to avoid a conflict of interest.

are solicitors really necessary?

Until May 1987, conveyancing for payment could only be undertaken by a qualified solicitor. Now it is lawful for 'licensed conveyancers' to undertake conveyancing and to set up in business alone or to work for solicitors' firms, estate agents, building societies and the like. The erosion of the solicitors' monopoly, and also the relaxation of their restrictions on advertising, has produced cut-price competition. As professional fees can vary greatly, it is worth shopping around for the best deal. Solicitors are obliged to charge only what is 'fair and reasonable'; the calculation of this sum does not include stamp duty and Land Registry fees and other unavoidable fees. It is wise to ask about 'hidden extras'.

There has never been anything to prevent 'do-it-yourself' conveyancing, but some people, especially solicitors, have always considered it a risky enterprise for laymen to embark on. At its more complicated, the process demands a knowledge of land law, trusts, planning and contract law. Although not beyond the abilities of the average layperson to undertake such a task, leasehold conveyancing is more complicated than its freehold counterpart. The covenants concerning repair and maintenance, ensuring that the buyer has the right to use common parts and services, and the payment of service charges are some of the points that need to be considered by the conveyancer.

At least if a professional makes a mistake, there will be insurance cover to redress the damage. All solicitors and licensed conveyancers must hold professional indemnity cover. If an individual makes a mistake, it could be extremely costly, even disastrous.

Mortgagees (building societies and banks, for example) will employ a professional conveyancer to represent their interests and the borrower has to pay the fee, so the savings in DIY conveyancing are not as great as might be expected.

finding out about the flat

Much needs to be discovered and discussed before buyer and seller are ready to enter into a contract: the obvious examples are the purchase price, the duration of the lease, the extent of the flat to be bought and what fixtures and fittings are to be left in the property.

The period before the contract also enables the buyer to sort out mortgage finance and allows certain essential information to be obtained.

preliminary enquiries

The buyer's legal adviser (the solicitor or conveyancer) makes what is known as 'preliminary enquiries' of the seller's solicitor or conveyancer by sending a standard printed form containing a set of formal questions and will also raise any additional queries which come from inspecting the documents or which are requested by the buyer. The questions cover much ground and include matters as to ownership of boundary walls, rights of others to cross the land, planning problems, mains services and disputes involving the property, for example.

As regards a flat, several specific questions appear on the form:

- does the seller own the freehold of the land or a leasehold estate?
- what are the names and addresses of the lessor(s) and to whom is ground rent paid?
- is the landlord's consent necessary for the sale and, if so, has it been obtained?
- have any covenants been broken?
- what services charges are payable?

There is a space on the form to allow extra questions to be asked (for example, concerning services provided, drainage and access to the flat, insurance of communal parts). Law stationers and local law societies publish special preliminary enquiry forms for use when buying a flat, designed to elicit information on sinking funds, the cost of past works and so on.

The answers received to all these questions may be unhelpful: 'inspection will show', 'please search', 'we cannot say' or 'not to the vendor's knowledge', and the point of the process can easily be side-stepped by the seller's solicitor. The questions themselves are not worded in plain english and may be difficult to understand by the layperson. Traditionally the answers are not guaranteed to be accurate (although some contracts now provide that the buyer can rely on replies to solicitor's preliminary enquiries). Any mistakes are unlikely to be discovered until after the purchase is completed.

Much can be achieved by the buyer himself inspecting the property and asking direct questions of the seller – for example, checking mains supplies and drainage, and discovering who lives in the property with the seller. Anyone who is over 18 years and living with the seller should be asked whether he or she has any rights over the property.

what is being let

The details of the premises contained in the estate agent's particulars will rarely be those contained in the lease. The tenant needs to ensure that he knows what he is buying. Potential problems which should be checked may concern the use of a garage, the extent of boundaries (parking rights, dust-bin areas, use of garden) the access to the premises and the rights to use common parts of the building (stairways, hallways and passages), type of central heating, number and type of lifts. These matters are usually raised on the preliminary enquiries made of the seller. A personal inspection of the property by the buyer will also help.

survey

If part of the money will come from a bank or building society, the lender will insist on a surveyor's valuation of the property before offering a mortgage advance. The fee for the valuation, based on the price of the property, has to be paid by the borrower. The valuation is, however, carried out on behalf of the lender, to find out whether the property is adequate security for the loan.

Valuation for mortgage purposes is not a structural survey, and does not guarantee that the property is worth the price asked for it.

Most building societies let the borrower see a copy of their valuation report but that is not the same as having your own structural survey done.

The surveyor who does the valuation for the lender can be asked to carry out a structural survey for the buyer at the same visit. (This saves time and money because the surveyor is already going to visit the property for the building society.) The fee can usually be negotiated and relates to the time taken to inspect the property and to write up the report.

In most cases, flat owners will have to contribute to the cost of repairs and maintenance – the ground floor tenant may be asked for contributions to the replacement of the roof. So, the survey should cover not only the flat itself but, ideally, an inspection of the whole building, including condition of the roof, foundations, drains, gutters and so on, also any communal services such as electricity, water or gas supplies.

local searches

A search will be made by the purchaser (or his legal adviser) of the local land charges register which is kept by the local authority. This is usually done by submitting a standard form (LLC 1) which asks for details of any local charges against the land. A further set of enquiries are made of the local authority (on form Con29). The questions relate to public matters such as planning permission, smokeless zones, compulsory purchase or local authority development affecting the area. The authority often replies by using a standard form of answers to the questionnaire.

The local search relates only to the property being bought. A personal inspection of the planning register kept by the local authority will reveal information about neighbouring property. It is advisable to make independent enquiries of the local authority and to see the local plan because this information will not be available on the formal search. The search will, of course, only reveal matters registered and not matters existing as proposals.

A personal search can be made by calling at the local authority's offices. This will avoid the long delay of waiting for the local authority to return the search form with replies. But the authority will not then give its official certificate, so there will be no compensation if there are any mistakes.

the evils of gazumping and contract races

It is still common for flat buyers to discover that they have been out-bid by a rival purchaser. As well as losing a desired residence, the unlucky buyer may have incurred considerable professional expenses: surveyors' costs, legal fees and fees concerning preliminary enquiries and local authority searches. To the buyer it may appear unjust that, in such circumstances, the seller is free to sell elsewhere for a better price. This situation arises because of one phrase which is commonly used in negotiations between seller and buyer: 'subject to contract'. This phrase ensures that negotiations which take place before a binding contract comes into existence lack any legal consequence.

The idea is to allow the buyer to avoid being legally

committed until the necessary legal and financial advice has been sought, but the procedure has been abused by sellers in order to make more money. Although gazumping is clearly an abuse, in fairness it must be recognised that buyers also abuse the 'subject to contract' provision by agreeing to buy a property without proper consideration and subsequently abandon the transaction either because they find a more suitable property or because, on reflection, they feel that it is unsuitable for their needs.

Proposals have been put forward that a pre-contract deposit should be taken from both parties and that this deposit should be forfeited if a party withdraws from the transaction without good cause. There is nothing to stop the parties arranging such a pre-contract deposit between themselves but, as yet, this is not widely done.

In a so-called contract race, the seller's solicitor sends a draft contract to the solicitors of several would-be buyers and the first to send it back, signed and with the necessary deposit, gets the flat. The Law Society has attempted to regulate this practice by obliging the seller's solicitor to disclose the existence of other prospective buyers to all the others. Not all solicitors fulfil this obligation and, in any event, it does not prevent gazumping, but it can give notice of the possibility to all the parties involved.

It is possible to take out insurance for financial loss arising from gazumping.

on to the next step

Several weeks will pass before the buyer knows the results of the searches and enquiries. If nothing untoward is revealed, buyer and seller will be ready to press on to the next stage and enter a legally binding agreement. Up to this stage, either party can withdraw from the transaction.

THE CONTRACT

A contract to grant or to assign a lease is governed by certain rules. Unless made in writing or, at the least, evidenced in writing, the contract is unenforceable at law by an action for breach of contract. It is important to realise that a contract which is perfectly valid may yet be unenforceable due to what lawyers call a defect in its form. The defect may be that the contract is not in writing on paper or does not spell out the necessary details. However, a buyer or seller who has acted to his own disadvantage or spent money on the faith of the contract – paid for repairs, for example – may apply to the court for the contract to be enforced. (This is what lawyers call the 'doctrine of part performance'.) Also, any deposit paid may be retained by the seller or reclaimed by the buyer.

This particular problem rarely arises in practice where the involvement of lawyers brings with it the drafting of a formal contract in writing.

what is in the contract

The contract is commonly typed on a standard form (either the National Conditions of Sale or the Law Society's Contract for Sale) which contains a large number of provisions. It incorporates both the particulars of sale and the conditions of sale. The particulars describe the subject matter of the contract (the description of the property, the nature of the lease to be sold and the benefits and burdens passing with the sale); the conditions state the terms on which the property is sold (provisions as to deposit, covenants, vacant possession, date for completion and insurance, for example). For the professional, it takes only a short time to fill in the blanks, delete irrelevant provisions, and add any special conditions required for that particular transaction.

In the case of a new lease being granted, the draft lease may be annexed to the contract. Or, where appropriate – namely when an existing lease is being assigned – there may be a draft deed of assignment annexed.

preparation of the contract

The contract is drafted by the seller's legal adviser and is sent, with an identical copy, to the buyer's legal adviser for amendment or approval. The terms of the contract may be further negotiated at this stage and it is not uncommon for the final draft of the contract to be quite different from that originally proposed. There may be much 'to-ing and fro-ing' between the solicitors to sort out such matters as the date of completion, the amount of the deposit to be paid, the wording of the covenants where a new lease is being created and any matters which the buyer wants included in the contract.

Once agreement has been reached, the buyer's legal adviser retains one copy of the draft and returns the other to the seller's who types the contract in its final form and sends one copy back to the buyer's legal adviser for checking. Both the parties – the buyer and the seller – will each sign their respective copy (both are identical) in readiness to exchange them. This should, of course, not be done until the buyer's building society, bank or other lenders made a mortgage offer. At exchange of contracts, the buyer commits himself to pay the full purchase price to the seller, and would be in great difficulties if the mortgage were to be refused.

fixtures

The buyer needs to know what items are to remain in the premises as part of the purchase price. An outgoing tenant, on assignment of a lease or at the end of it, will need to be sure what can be removed. Items which may raise problems include fitted carpets, kitchen units, double glazing, gas fires and light fittings, for example. The solution to such problems turns on whether the items are fixtures or not. If the articles are attached to the building (screwed in, nailed down, or plumbed in) and were brought there in order to improve it, they will generally be regarded as fixtures and not to be removed. This rule of thumb is not conclusive, however: if fixing the item (a heavy painting, for example) to the wall is the only means by which it can be enjoyed, it will remain a 'chattel' and not become a fixture. Items which are not fixtures may be taken away at will unless the contract specifically mentions them as staying behind.

The purpose for which an item was introduced on the premises is a key factor. A tenant may remove fittings during or at the end of the lease only if they are ornamental and domestic in nature. Ornamental and domestic would cover boilers, cookers, mirrors and mantelpieces for example. Mantelpieces being removed by a departing tenant would be unusual unless the mantelpiece was of considerable artistic value. If a mantelpiece is part of the architectural style of the room, it must not be removed. When an item is removed, any damage caused to the property should be made good and this may involve some re-decoration work. The tenant may, otherwise, be liable to compensate either the landlord or the assignee of the lease.

However, the tenant would not be entitled to remove fitted wardrobes, showers and doors, for example. Such items are clearly intended to become fixtures and cannot be classified as ornamental and domestic.

Unless the contract states otherwise, the fixtures are paid for as part of the purchase price. The seller can insert a provision in the contract whereby the buyer pays an extra sum for items which the seller would be entitled to remove but is leaving behind.

Because the rules about what is and what is not removable are confusing, it is important for the buyer (and seller) to be clear what is included in the price, what will be removed, and what will be left behind but at a separate price. It is useful to have an inventory annexed to the contract detailing the items to be paid for by the buyer, and their prices.

A well-drawn contract should mention all the doubtful items and not simply leave them to be covered by "fixtures".

exchange of contracts

The formal contract becomes binding only when the parts which have been signed are exchanged so that the buyer has a contract signed by the seller, and the seller has an identical document signed by the buyer. Exchange is the vital stage which brings the contract into existence.

Where a buyer is in a 'chain' of transactions, it is necessary to try to synchronise all exchanges on the same date. It would be disastrous to exchange contracts for the purchase of a flat and then find that the potential buyer of your present property withdraws at the last minute.

The exchange can be ceremonial (the solicitors or even the buyer and seller meet and hand over their, or their client's signed document), or by post (the more usual method). It is also common between solicitors to 'exchange contracts' by telephone.

Where the buyer or the seller does not have a solicitor, exchange of contracts is usually better done in person so as to be certain any related sale or purchase is also concluded contemporaneously.

the effect of the contract

Once a valid and enforceable contract is in existence after exchange of contracts, the seller is regarded as holding the property in trust for the buyer. Although the legal title remains with the seller, the 'beneficial ownership' is regarded as having passed to the buyer. The consequences of this somewhat mystifying notion may prove important:

○ the seller must still manage and preserve the property and is liable to the buyer for any failure to carry out necessary repairs or maintenance. There is, however, no obligation to make improvements;
○ the seller has the right to retain possession until the property is conveyed to the buyer and remains liable for all running expenses until that time;
○ the risk is regarded as having passed to the buyer. This means that if the flat is damaged or destroyed, for example, the loss lies on the shoulders of the buyer and not the seller. The buyer still has to pay over the purchase price, even if he will not get the flat in return. It is, therefore, crucial that the buyer insures the premises from the day of exchange of contracts. If the landlord

insures, the buyer's interest must be noted on the policy from the date of exchange of contracts;

○ the buyer can benefit from any increase in the value of the flat pending completion of the transaction – for example, an increase in the market value due to planning permission being obtained.

The contract commits both parties to the transfer of the property. The buyer will, however, still need to ensure that the seller has a good title and that there are no third party rights adversely affecting the property.

checking on the seller's right to sell

There are two systems of land transfer in operation, unregistered and registered. The registered system now covers over 87% of England and Wales so that it is likely that the flat will be within an area where the registered system is in operation.

For the present purpose, the main difference between the two systems lies in the manner by which the seller's title to the property is proved.

In the unregistered system, the process of what is called deducing the seller's title is by an examination of the title deeds to the property.

The registered system is more efficient and staightfor-ward: ownership is guaranteed when the seller's name is entered on the official register of title. The buyer's legal adviser needs only to make a search at the Land Registry and check that the seller's name is entered on the proprietor-ship register. A copy of the entry on the register should have already been forwarded to the buyer with the draft con-tracts, but it is possible that it might be out of date. A check must, therefore, be made to ensure that there have been no other entries either registered since exchanging contracts or which were not provided for in the contract.

pre-completion steps

A prospective tenant does not have the automatic right to examine the landlord's freehold title and make sure, amongst other things, that the landlord has the right to grant the lease. Without this, it would prove very difficult or even impossible to obtain a mortgage and, subsequently, to sell the lease. A provision should, therefore, always be inserted into the contract allowing this investigation. An assignee cannot rely on this contractual provision between the freeholder and the original tenant, but will experience no problem because the freeholder's title has previously been established.

unregistered
If the title to the property is unregistered, the buyer of a new lease must secure from the seller evidence of the latter's title to the property. In relation to the freehold title of the landlord, this will take the form of title deeds which disclose all dealings with the property during, at least, the previous 15 years. Lawyers call this an 'abstract of title'; it often consists of one or two conveyances and, sometimes, includes a typed summary.

On the assignment of an existing lease, the buyer should ensure that the contract provides for him to have the right to investigate the assignor's title, and this should be done.

The assignee's building society, bank or other mortgagee will also check the seller's or assignor's title.

registered
In the registered system, until the new Land Registration Act 1988 comes into force, the prospective tenant will need the authority of the landlord to make a search, at the Land Registry, of the registered title to the property. A prospective assignee of a registered lease is similarly able, with the seller's consent, to see the register at the Land Registry containing the details of the lease which is to be assigned.

both registered and unregistered
The buyer's legal adviser will search the Land Charges Register (there is no need for authorisation) or Land Register (the authority of the seller is required), whichever is appropriate (the former for unregistered, the latter for registered property), in order to discover whether the property is bound by any rights of a third party which have not previously been disclosed. These pre-completion searches are made by sending a form to the appropriate body and awaiting the reply.

if something comes to light

If an entry has been made, the buyer should, generally, require it to be cleared before going ahead with the transaction. This the seller will not be able to do where the rights protected by registration are those of third parties. In such a case, he would be in breach of contract if he had failed to specify in the contract that the property is subject to these rights. The buyer would be well advised to withdraw from the contract and claim back his deposit.

If any defect in the title emerges or any rights which adversely affect the property are discovered, the buyer will make further enquiries (known as 'requisitions') of the seller. If the defect is not rectified or the matter not clarified satisfactorily, the buyer will, usually, be able to withdraw from the transaction. The requisitions are contained on a printed form and will include statements that on completion vacant possession of the flat will be given and that any existing mortgages will be discharged, provided the contract so provides.

Withdrawal and liability for misrepresentation are considered later in the book.

the deposit

A deposit has to be provided by the buyer on exchange of contracts. The deposit is normally 10% of the total purchase price but some sellers may be willing to accept a lesser deposit.

If the buyer withdraws from the transaction without good reason, the seller may keep the deposit; if it is the seller who is in default, the buyer can sue for the recovery of the money. (There is statutory provision for the court to order the return of the deposit in cases where it is fair and just to do so, but this power will rarely be exercised in relation to the default of the buyer of a long residential lease.)

The deposit, therefore, has several purposes: it is part-payment for the property and a guarantee for the seller, and it is an incentive for the buyer to keep to the bargain.

Failure to pay the deposit (or the cheque not being met on presentation) is regarded by the court as a fundamental breach of contract, entitling the seller to withdraw from the contract.

stakeholder or agent?

Where the deposit is paid to the seller's solicitor, it is generally better to ensure that it is to be held as 'stakeholder' and not 'agent for the seller'. A stakeholder cannot release the deposit to the seller until completion and it must be kept safely in a deposit account. The stakeholder can, however, keep the interest on the money, subject to agreement.

Sometimes – and particularly for first-time buyers who are getting a 95% or 100% mortgage, or for people buying and selling whose money is always tied up in the property – it is difficult to find a 10% deposit.

There are two main ways round this problem, each of which has disadvantages, but which allow the buyer to avoid taking a bridging loan for 10% of the value of the property he is buying, with the extra expenses of arrangement fees and high interest charges this entails.

The first is that a seller may accept a 5% deposit if he is allowed to hold it as 'agent for the vendor', in the contract. This would not usually be acceptable, but where the seller's solicitor gives an undertaking to the buyer or his solicitor that the deposit will only be used and released by him for the purpose of a deposit on the seller's dependent sale, the buyer has the security that the money is still 'in the system' and has not simply been paid over to the seller personally.

The question as to whether the deposit is to be held as stakeholder or agent needs to be resolved during the drafting of the contract. In practice, deposits are often held by solicitors as the seller's agent, to enable the money to be used as deposit by the seller on the property he is buying. Adopting the agency system makes it easier for 'chains' to be successfully negotiated, since a single deposit by the person at the bottom of the chain will in practice be used as the deposit for all the other links.

It does not in any way alter the liability of the seller to repay the deposit if he defaults. If the circumstances are such that the seller is not himself entitled to the return of the deposit on his own purchase contract, the buyer would have to sue his seller for the deposit. The converse problem can arise for the person accepting the deposit on these terms if he has to return a deposit to his buyer but cannot obtain the return of the deposit from his own seller.

The easiest situation remains that each pays 10% to be held as stakeholders – but many people now prefer to obtain the 'cash flow' advantages of avoiding this.

deposit guarantee schemes

The second way of dealing with the problem of deposits is that solicitors (and other professional advisers) may be able to arrange, for a premium (say £60–£200 depending on the sum of the deposit required) to be paid for an insurance policy which avoids a deposit being paid altogether. All the buyer has to pay, on exchanging contracts, is the premium. This is, however, non-returnable (nor can the amount paid be deducted from the purchase price payable on completion as is the case with a deposit).

The terms of the insurance policy are that it is issued to the seller, and the insurance company will pay to the seller the amount of the 10% deposit if circumstances arise entitling the seller to keep the deposit, had it been paid. In this event, the insurance company will have the right to reclaim the full amount from the buyer.

This is a fairly new development in conveyancing practice and there is therefore as yet no realistic track record of how easily the insurance company will pay out on the policy and what its requirements will be to admit the claim. Sellers are often reluctant to accept such a policy (nor can a deposit guarantee be passed along the chain, as a money-deposit can).

completion

Completion takes place when the buyer pays over the balance of the purchase money and the seller hands over the relevant title deeds (for unregistered property) or land certificate and lease (for registered property). If unregistered, the buyer becomes the legal owner of the property at this time.

In the registered system of conveyancing, the legal title passes to the buyer when his name is entered in the Land Register, in place of the seller's name. The buyer's solicitor will have to send to the Land Registry an application form with the relevant documents. Because registration takes so long, the date on which the buyer's application for registration is received by the Registry is the operative date.

Completion takes place, normally within four weeks of the exchange of contracts, at the seller's legal adviser's office. If keys are being held by an estate agent, the seller will authorise their release at this stage.

mortgagees and completion

Completion of the transaction involves, essentially, the passing over of the purchase price and, in return, the receiving of the title deeds or land certificate and lease relating to the flat.

Generally, however, the situation is complicated because the flat being sold will be subject to the seller's mortgage and the buyer will be assisted by a mortgage advance. The seller's mortgagee will have possession of the deeds, or charge certificate and lease, and will release them only when the existing mortgage is paid off. The buyer's mortgagee will hand over the money only when receiving the deeds or land certificate and the mortgage deed signed by the buyer. At the end of the completion process, the following has usually occurred:

○ the seller's mortgagee leaves with a banker's draft needed to clear the seller's mortgage and will give an undertaking to do so within a couple of weeks;

○ the seller's solicitor has a banker's draft for the balance of the sale price;

○ the buyer can go home to a new flat;

○ the buyer's mortgagee gets custody of the deeds or charge certificate and lease, and the mortgage deed, after the formalities of stamping and registration have been attended to by the buyer's solicitor.

ARRANGING A MORTGAGE

A mortgage is a major form of credit. Strictly speaking, the word does not mean a loan but security provided by the borrower. The individual is enabled to buy a home with the help of the loan while offering the property he has bought as security for that loan. The lender of money (the mortgagee) is given a valuable form of security in the property bought by the borrower (the mortgagor). The majority of residential properties are financed by a mortgage. In the old days, the lion's share of the market went to the building societies. Now the institutional lenders include building societies, banks, local authorities, insurance companies and others.

the dream of home ownership . . .
The mortgage is the largest financial commitment in the lives of most people. By offering a house or flat as security for the loan, the buyer is able to borrow a substantial sum which is repayable over a long period of years (generally 25 or 30 years). The benefit of this indebtedness is that the borrower has the opportunity to become an owner-occupier in circumstances in which it would otherwise be impossible. The mortgagor acquires a place to live and, at the same time, makes a capital investment. Even though the buyer owes the lender the amount borrowed and secures this by way of the whole property, when the property goes up in value this increase all belongs to the buyer and does not increase the amount owed. Except for very rare types of 'equity' mortgages, the lender does not acquire a share in the property.

... *and the nightmare*

Notwithstanding the buoyancy of the mortgage market, there is a dramatic and disturbing increase in the number of mortgage defaults. In 1985, there were over 65,000 default actions taken to the courts, 49,600 borrowers were known to be 6 to 12 months in arrears with their repayments and 10% of people adjudged homeless were so as a consequence of a court order for mortgage default. These figures do not include the high number of cases where the property was voluntarily surrendered to the mortgagee. While redundancy and long term unemployment remain facts of life, the situation is unlikely to improve even if mortgagees make the qualifying conditions more stringent.

One of the lessons to potential borrowers is not to overextend themselves financially. People contemplating a mortgage should find out how much it is going to cost them each month and satisfy themselves in advance that they will be able to continue paying for it. It is possible to take out insurance for redundancy and ill health (but the premiums are high).

bank, building society or other lender

With the emergence of the high-street banks into the mortgage market, and increased competition, potential home-buyers have a wide choice of institutions from which to borrow. There is little to choose between banks and building societies and many offer various incentives, such as fixed interest rates as an option for the first few years of the loan, or specially tailored schemes for professional people.

It has become possible, in many cases, to obtain a so-called mortgage certificate, even before the property has been found, which states how much the lender is willing to lend, subject to the value of the property to be bought, based on the financial status of the potential borrower. Many institutional lenders have relaxed the once rigid 'two-and-a-half times the gross income' calculation for the maximum loan. Some mortagees are more generous than others in this calculation and also as regards the earnings of a co-purchaser (spouse, friend or flat-mate, for example). Most lenders will advance between 90% and 95% of the purchase price, subject to valuation, and special facilities (albeit expensive) are available for borrowers who need 'top-up' finance. But borrowers' personal circumstances may make it unwise to take up a mortgage offer that would stretch them too much financially.

Although more flats are normally found in or around large towns, rural bank or building society branches also have experience with leasehold purchases, so it should not be more difficult to obtain the necessary finance for buying a flat than for buying a house. But it must be remembered that a lease is a dwindling asset. It is clear that shorter leases (say between 40 and 60 years) and older properties are unattractive to many mortgagees. They do not offer sufficient security for the loan (nor may they be a good investment for the buyer).

It is advisable to 'shop around' and check out the various offers and schemes available. (There are frequent *Which?* reports dealing with mortgages; a recent one was published in April 1988).

If real problems arise about the property or the borrower's financial situation, the engagement of a mortgage broker or insurance broker may prove helpful. There should be no charge or fee for the borrower if he takes out an endowment mortgage.

repayment, endowment or pension mortgage?

A repayment mortgage is one under which the interest and capital are paid off at a monthly rate throughout the duration of the mortgage.

An endowment mortgage also involves monthly payments to the lender, but only of the interest on the loan, without any instalment repayments of the capital. That will be repaid all in one lump sum at the end of the mortgage term. Under this type of mortgage, the borrower has to take out a life assurance policy which will guarantee the payment of the mortgage debt either on death or when the policy matures (in say, 25 or 30 years) and assign the policy to the lender, as security. The policy involves a further monthly premium payment, to the insurance company.

As to which of these two types of mortgage is the more advantageous, there is no certain answer. Under the repayment scheme, the borrower may be required also to take out life assurance cover. It would be a cheaper type, a so-called term insurance in which the policy is only of the duration of the mortgage and the capital payment is made only if the insured person should die before the mortgage is repaid; there is, therefore, no capital sum payable on the maturity of the policy. It is a decreasing term insurance: the amount payable under the policy becomes less and less as the term goes on so that it matches the mortgage capital outstanding. It is therefore considerably cheaper than endowment assurance where the full amount of the loan remains outstanding.

The monthly payments used to be marginally lower with a repayment mortgage but this is not now necessarily so. With a repayment mortgage, there is no investment involved. An endowment mortgage coupled with a with-profits insurance policy can prove a shrewd investment in the long term; it is also possible to link the mortgage to a low-cost policy. If you are going to sell your flat again before the insurance policy matures, the same policy can be used for the next endowment mortgage and if a greater amount of loan is needed for the next house or flat, an additional policy taken out. But if you need to cash in a policy within a short time, it would not be a good investment.

In any event, it is important that the borrower shops around for a company with a proven track record for investment and does not merely rely on the company recommended by the lender (unless the lender is an independent adviser under the Financial Services Act 1986).

A pension mortgage is another possibility. It used not to be appropriate for most borrowers, and only relevant for self-employed people around or over the age of 35 years. With the increase in private pension schemes, as part of the background to the introduction of the personal pensions system in July 1988, this type of mortgage is likely to become more popular.

With a pension mortgage, the borrower arranges for a mortgage loan alongside a suitable pension policy (and sometimes a life assurance policy as well). During the term of the loan, the borrower pays only the interest due each month and no capital repayment is made. The premiums paid under the pension scheme generate a (tax free) cash sum that is ultimately used to pay off the mortgage debt and also provide for a pension for life which is taxed as earned income.

Although somewhat similar to an endowment mortgage, a pension mortgage is more tax efficient because of the tax relief on the premiums paid into the pension scheme. The borrower should, however, be aware that the lump sum used for repayment of the mortgage loan reduces the capital available on which the pension is based, so that the pension will be a reduced one.

formality of creating a mortgage

There are two ways by which a legal mortgage of leasehold property can arise.

One of them is convoluted and artificial: the borrower grants the lender a sublease of the property subject to the stipulation that this sublease will end on the repayment of the mortgage debt. The borrower remains in occupation throughout and retains the full legal title to the property. This method of mortgage creation is not commonly found.

The simpler, more straightforward and usual method has a more complicated technical name: it is known as a 'charge by deed, expressed to be by way of a legal mortgage'. All that is required is a deed which contains a statement that the property is subject to the mortgage.

The position of the borrower and the lender is, essentially, the same no matter which way the mortgage is created. In practice, the majority of lenders use the charge method.

the terms of the mortgage deed

Conveyancing solicitors should explain to their clients the consequences of entering a mortgage because the mortgage documents themselves are unhelpful. Mortgage documentation differs widely in structure and content, and no standardised form is yet available.

Apart from the details as to the repayment of the loan, there are various obligations imposed on the borrower. The standard terms incorporated into mortgage deeds include these conditions:

○ to keep the property in good and sufficient repair and to permit the mortgagee to enter and examine the condition of the premises;
○ to carry out repairs and remedy defects as specified by the lender. It may be that the mortgagee will retain part of the loan until such work is undertaken;
○ to obtain the consent of the lender before structural alterations and extensions are carried out;
○ to insure the property for fire risks and deposit the policy with the mortgagee. The borrower will also be obliged to inform the lender when claims arise under the policy, and to comply with any reasonable requirement as to the use of any sums paid out under a claim. Where there is a policy for the whole block of flats, taken out by the landlord, the mortgagee will require its interest to be endorsed on the policy;
○ to sublet the premises only with the prior consent of the lender;
○ to comply with all the provisions of the lease;
○ to allow the lender, at the expense of the borrower, to perform any obligation which the latter has failed to perform with the right to enter the premises, on seven day's notice, to ensure the obligation is satisfied.

In case of non-payment by the borrower, the lender will have the right of taking possession of the property. (This is dealt with later in the book.)

The mortgage debt can be paid off prematurely only if written notice is given to the mortgagee who may ask for what is known as a 'redemption' fee. Penalties for early redemption may be the equivalent of three or six months' interest, regardless of notice given, but in practice an early redemption fee is not usually claimed nowadays.

The borrower has to pay all costs and expenditure the lender incurs (for example, legal expenses of investigating the seller's title at the conveyancing stage and, should the need arise, of legal action on default or the cost of the premiums if the borrower fails to take out insurance cover).

the borrower's rights

Such protection as is offered to the borrower may prove invaluable in a time of economic depression.

The right to redeem the mortgage at any time after the date stipulated for redemption in the mortgage deed (normally 6 months after the creation of the mortgage) cannot be excluded, unreasonably postponed, or restricted by any other contractual terms. Redemption takes place when the capital, interest and any agreed redemption fee are paid in full.

The rate of interest charged is not fixed throughout the duration of the loan and fluctuates, both upwards and downwards, as deemed necessary by the mortgagee. Although it is necessary that lenders should be free to alter the interest rates to suit the economic climate, the courts have the jurisdiction to set aside an increase if it is oppressive and harsh. This is unlikely to be relevant in a building society or bank mortgage: it is almost inconceivable that normal building society rates would be held to be harsh, but it may apply to fringe lenders.

The Consumer Credit Act 1974 contains a number of miscellaneous provisions which affect certain mortgages. However, the Act does not apply to specified bodies such as building societies, local authorities, banks and insurance companies and only has relevance to sums of less than £15,000. While the Consumer Credit Act does not enter into the mainstream residential mortgage, it is important as regards fringe lenders, and to second mortgages which are often serviced by the non-institutional credit companies. Such sources of credit are often used by people who cannot obtain finance from the usual high-street sources.

tax relief

A major incentive for buying property with the help of a mortgage is that income tax relief is available on the interest paid on a loan of up to £30,000 used for the purpose of buying property for owner-occupancy.

Under mortgage interest relief at source (MIRAS), the relief at basic rate of tax is deducted from the monthly payments made to the lender. Tax relief at higher rates will be dealt with through an increased PAYE code or, for the self-employed, by registration with the tax inspector.

Only one tax relief on a £30,000 loan is available to the purchaser of the property. Where there are co-purchasers and flat sharers, it can be divided between them (but not £30,000 each).

Tax relief used to be, but is no longer, available on home improvement loans.

the lender's protection

The lender will ensure that the legal title to the property, which is to form the security for the loan, is sound and reliable. Institutional mortgagees usually engage the services of the buyer's solicitor (provided the firm is on the building society's/bank's panel of solicitors) to investigate the title for them. The purpose of this investigation is to make sure that the buyer is getting what is being paid for and also to discover whether any rights belonging to third parties adversely affect the property. This protects the lenders' interests should they have to call up the loan. The cost of this exercise has to be met by the borrower. The solicitor charges for acting both for the buyer and for the lender, but this usually works out cheaper than where the lender has a separate solicitor acting.

The lender will take and keep the title deeds, or ensure that the mortgage is registered at the Land Registry and keep the charge certificate. This prevents the property being dealt with (remortgaged or sold) but makes it easy to sell it if the borrower defaults.

The mortgagee has the right to insure the property for fire, at the mortgagor's expense, or insist that the borrower does so. (The premiums may be charged as an addition to the mortgage debt and, therefore, interest has to be paid on them throughout the loan.) This right is implied into every mortgage deed, and the lender usually requires more comprehensive coverage to be taken out by the mortgagor personally, as a condition of the loan, and the policy to be deposited with the mortgagee. But the lender has no right to any sums paid out under such personally-taken policies.

council housing's right-to-buy mortgages

Various statutory provisions give local authorities a power (in some cases a duty) to sell council property (freehold or leasehold) to tenants and the tenants have the right to a mortgage in order to finance the transaction. The mortgage is repayable over a period of up to 25 years. Each prospective buyer has an individual income limit, although a local authority may, if appropriate, advance a sum greater than this income would normally warrant. The detailed calculations of the income limits are in accordance with regulations prescribed by the secretary of state.

The subject of council tenants' right to buy is briefly summarised later in the book.

drip mortgages

This is a method of home buying more properly known as a rental purchase. It is technically not a mortgage and is a scheme akin to buying a home on hire purchase. In essence, it consists of a contract for the sale of the property, with the buyer occupying the premises and paying the purchase price by instalments. Legal title to the property is conveyed to the borrower only on the final payment.

This form of credit is generally used in the context of low-quality, low-priced housing. The borrower is particularly vulnerable as the protection offered by law to the mainstream mortgagor is unavailable. An occupier could, therefore, be evicted for non-payment, losing both a home and the rental payments already made. The drip mortgage is often used to avoid the Rent Act protection afforded to tenants of rented property and is the source of much abuse. It should be treated with great caution.

SUMMARY OF A TYPICAL TRANSACTION

- Seller finds buyer either privately or through an estate agent.

- Buyer and seller (usually) instruct their respective legal advisers (solicitor or licensed conveyancer).

- Buyer arranges mortgage finance, if needed.

- Seller's legal adviser gets ready a draft contract. Draft contract describes the property to be sold and rights and obligations that go with it, and states duration of lease, price and covenants.

- Draft contract is approved by buyer's legal adviser.

- Buyer arranges for survey of property; obtains mortgage offer, if appropriate.

- Buyer's legal adviser makes formal enquiries (re the property) of the seller and of the local authority (re surroundings), makes a local land charges search and should inspect the property.

- Both buyer and seller agree to the contract as drafted and are ready to enter a legally binding contract to buy and to sell the flat; this is done by an exchange of contracts. Buyer provides a deposit (usually 10% of price).

- If the title is unregistered, seller's legal adviser sends details of recent deeds of the property; if the title is registered, sends authority to inspect the register (from 1989, inspection open to all, without need for authority).

- Buyer's legal adviser examines title documents to ensure that buyer will get what is expected. If anything needs clarification, makes enquiries of the seller.

- If there is a mortgage offer, solicitor for the lender (usually the same as acting for the buyer) also investigates the seller's title documents.

- Buyer's legal adviser makes searches to discover any rights of a third party over the property. For unregistered title, search is of the Land Charges register; if registered, search is made at the District Land Registry.

- The lease (or the assignment of lease) is drafted, embodying the relevant terms of the contract, and when approved by both parties, final copy is typed.

- If mortgage finance is involved, lender prepares mortgage deed to be signed by the buyer.

- Completion takes place. Buyer pays the balance of purchase price and seller provides the title deeds (if unregistered) or land certificate (if registered). The lender (where appropriate) takes the documents and the mortgage deed in return for providing the mortgage funds. If unregistered property, buyer acquires legal ownership of it on completion. If title to the flat is registered, the lease has to be registered at the Land Registry before legal ownership passes to buyer.

- The lease or assignment is produced to the Inland Revenue, by buyer's legal adviser, and any necessary stamp duty paid.

BREACH OF CONTRACT, BEFORE COMPLETION AND AFTERWARDS

Where a breach of contract or a misrepresentation within the contract arises, the aggrieved party has various options. These are: to withdraw from the contract ('rescission'), to force an unwilling party to complete, to claim compensation (or damages, the words are interchangeable) or, after completion has taken place, to claim rescission or compensation.

withdrawing from the contract (rescission)

Refusing to complete, that is withdrawing from the contract, may be permissible when there has been misrepresentation or breach of contract, or under a specific provision in the contract.

what is misrepresentation?

When a statement of fact is made (for example about access to the property, or car parking, or use of garden) on which the buyer relies and which turns out to be untrue, this is a misrepresentation.

A misrepresentation in a pre-contract statement may be fraudulent, negligent or innocent.

A *fraudulent* misrepresentation is one which is known to

be false or is made recklessly. The buyer may withdraw from the contract and/or claim compensation for the amounts he has lost.

A *negligent* misrepresentation is one where the person who made it has no reasonable grounds for believing in its accuracy nor caring about it. The buyer can withdraw from the contract and/or claim compensation.

An *innocent* misrepresentation is neither fraudulent nor negligent and refers to a genuine mistake. There is no right to compensation, but the buyer may be allowed to withdraw from the contract.

Rescission is a 'discretionary remedy' and therefore the approval of the court is needed before the buyer can lawfully withdraw from the contract. The court may award damages in lieu of rescission in the case of negligent and innocent misrepresentation.

Where the contract uses the National Conditions of Sale or the Law Society's Contract for Sale, the right to rescind (that is withdraw from the contract) may be restricted. The Law Society's general conditions, for example, state that:

> ". . . no error, omission or misstatement . . . in . . . any statement made in the course of negotiations leading to the contract shall annul the sale or entitle the purchaser to be discharged from the purchase."

Rescission is allowed under these Conditions where compensation is thought by the court to be insufficient (an example would be where it is incorrectly stated that a garage is included in the lease) or where the misrepresentation makes the property substantially different from that described in the contract.

The National Conditions deprive the buyer of the right to rescind unless the statement was made fraudulently or prevents the buyer getting substantially what was intended to be bought.

The standard answers to the buyer's preliminary enquiries are not guaranteed to be accurate and, generally, will not constitute a misrepresentation. Where the contract provides that answers of the seller's solicitors to the buyer's standard preliminary enquiries may be relied upon as accurate, they could however constitute a (mis)representation. In practice, such replies tend therefore to be very general and non-committal in their nature.

breach of contract

If there is a serious breach of the contract, the other party may be able to withdraw from it and claim compensation. This may arise, for example, where the seller is unable to convey what was contracted (for example the seller does not have title, or vacant possession cannot be given) or where the time for completion was stipulated and made 'of the essence' (that is, completion time is stated to have become an essential term of the contract) and has since passed.

If there is a substantial misdescription in the contract (for example, as to the physical area of the flat), the buyer cannot be forced to complete the contract and can claim compensation and recover any deposit paid. If the misdescription is not substantial and of a minor nature (for example, a less serious mistake in the description of the flat), the buyer could get only compensation and would be obliged to go through with the transaction.

Time is not usually of the essence in relation to the completion date, but can be made so if one party serves on the other a 'notice to complete'. Following this notice, if a party fails to complete by the date specified, this will constitute a breach of contract and allow the other to withdraw and claim compensation.

rescission under a specific provision

The contract may allow a party to withdraw from the
agreement on the occurrence of stated circumstances. The
Law Society's conditions, for example, allow a buyer to
rescind within 4 weeks of exchange of contracts if some
matter comes to light (perhaps a compulsory purchase
order or road development) which would reduce the value
of the property. But these rights are usually excluded by
special conditions written into the contract.

what happens on rescission

The contract will usually specify the consequences of
withdrawal (under the Law Society's conditions, for
example, the seller repays the deposit and the buyer returns
all documents which have been forwarded, copies of the
title deeds and the proposed lease or assignment).

enforcing completion

If a buyer (or seller) cannot withdraw from the contract, but
is reluctant to proceed, the other party can apply to the court
for 'specific performance', that is an order requiring the
contract to be performed, or can serve a notice to complete.

specific performance

This is a discretionary remedy which is only granted by the
court when compensation is not sufficient. In relation to the
sale of a house or flat, specific performance is usually
granted.

notice to complete

A notice to complete makes time of the essence. The Law Society's conditions provide that a completion notice can be served at any time after the contractual completion date has passed and the notice must give at least 21 days in which to complete.

If completion does not take place by the time stated in the notice, the aggrieved party can treat the contract as at an end, sue for compensation, and re-sell the property (if he is a seller) or buy other property (if the buyer).

compensation

Where completion does not take place, the aggrieved party can recover for loss which can be considered as reasonably arising in the normal course of events as a result of such a breach of contract. For the seller, this may include the difference between the contract price of the property and the current market value; expenses of re-selling; interest on outstanding purchase money from the contractual completion date (the standard conditions stipulate the rate of interest). For the buyer, compensation may be based on the difference between the market value of the property at the date of the breach and the contract price; also legal expenses and survey fees, for example.

after completion
A misrepresentation or mistake may emerge after the completion of the contract. For example, the buyer completes and then discovers that a sitting tenant is in the flat. The contractual term to give vacant possession has been broken and the buyer should try to rescind the contract. But

rescission is unlikely to be granted after completion because the buyer's mortgagee would be prejudicially affected: it would be considered unfair on the bank or building society which has advanced the mortgage money to lose the security for the loan. The buyer can, however, claim compensation. The compensation will be the difference between the value of the flat with vacant possession and its value with a sitting tenant.

THE LEASE

It may be said that lawyers have two major failings; one is that they do not write well and the other is that they think they do. Nowhere is this clearer than in conveyancing documentation. A lease is a highly technical document, littered with expressions carefully chosen and yet which often remain unintelligible for the lay person. The tradition of not using punctuation also helps to confuse matters.

The creation of a lease or of an underlease, and the assignment of an existing lease, all follow a similar pattern. Apart from some minor cosmetic changes, the form of the lease in registered land normally follows the structure used in the unregistered system.

drafting and finalising the contents of the lease

After exchange, the lease is initially put into draft form by the landlord's (the seller's) solicitors and will follow one of the many standard forms, adapted to suit the individual characteristics of the parties and the premises. The structure and content of one lease may vary greatly from others.

The lease as proposed is submitted (generally at the same time as the draft contract) to the buyer's solicitor for approval. Amendments can be made to the draft if appropriate (about price, ground rent, covenants and terms of the lease) and a final form will be agreed. The lease as finalised will be put into deed form (which means it is typed out nicely, ready to have a seal in the form of a small red disc affixed to it), duplicated by the buyer's solicitor and each party provided with a copy.

further steps

The lease is forwarded to the Inland Revenue for stamping and, in the unregistered system, there are no more formal steps to take. The tenant's mortgagee will require an undertaking from the solicitor that the lease will be sent as soon as possible. The lease will be kept in the safe custody of the mortgagee until the mortgage is paid off. When the lease is next sold, the next buyer will be able to inspect the original lease at the mortgagee's solicitor's office or have a copy of it forwarded to him (there will be a charge for this).

If the land is registered, for a lease or assignment for a term of more than 21 years, the transaction is only completed when the buyer becomes the registered proprietor of the lease and a land certificate is issued to prove it.

stamp duty

Stamp duty is a tax payable to the government on some deeds and documents, including deeds of assignment or conveyances. A lease, sublease or assignment may therefore attract stamp duty. At present, property up to and including the value of £30,000 is exempt. To take advantage of the exemption, a certificate of value must be incorporated into the lease. This certifies that the value paid for the property does not exceed £30,000. On property exceeding £30,000 stamp duty of 1% on the whole sum has to be paid. For example, the stamp duty on a flat costing £50,000 will be £500. Deeds and documents cannot be used as evidence or registered at the Land Registry unless they are properly stamped.

In addition, extra duty may be payable according to the length of the lease (less than 7 years, less than 100 years, over 100 years) and the amount of the annual rent. This aspect of stamp duty is very complicated. The Inland Revenue publish a scale from which the amount can be ascertained. As most long residential leases for flats carry nothing more than a low ground rent, this will not affect most buyers.

The rates for both aspects of the duty change from time to time. A solicitor should have up to date information about current stamp duty.

excluding fixtures

Fixtures are part of the property and, therefore, are included in the price for the lease. It is possible that the seller could 'sever' the fixtures and sell them to the buyer separately. This could lead to some saving on stamp duty.

EXAMPLE:

A flat is valued at £32,000 and will attract stamp duty on the whole amount at 1%. The flat contains carpets, kitchen units etc. which are valued at £2,000. If the contract stipulates that the buyer is to buy the items at £2,000, the value of the flat falls to £30,000 and is, therefore, exempt from stamp duty. This saves the buyer £320.

But it needs to be a genuine transaction and must not involve an artificially inflated figure.

the function of the lease

The lease is important because it will state the rights of the parties at the start of the tenancy and govern the future relationship between landlord and tenant from then on.

The tenant will need to be sure that the premises can be used as intended and that the obligations imposed by the lease will not outweigh the enjoyment of living in the property.

The landlord will seek to make sure that the tenant will not cause any nuisance or annoyance and will look after the premises.

The clearer the terms of the lease, the less the scope for disagreement. Leases are usually lengthy documents, often containing several schedules of terms.

a specimen lease

In the following abridged example, the covenants by the parties and some other provisions of the lease have been omitted. Such terms will be contained in lengthy schedules at the end of the lease.

The Lease made the 4th day of January 1988 **Between** Desmond Jackson of 23, Paris Avenue, Newcastle (hereafter called 'the landlord' which expression shall where the context so admits include the person for the time being entitled to the reversion immediately expectant on the determination of the term hereby granted) and Mary Rogers of 19 Poolfield Road, Newcastle (hereafter called 'the tenant' which expression shall where the context so admits include her successors in title)
Witnesseth as follows:
In consideration of the sum of £50,000 paid by the tenant to the landlord (the receipt whereof the landlord hereby acknowledges), the rent reserved and tenants covenants hereinafter contained the landlord **Hereby Demises** unto the tenant **All those** premises known as Flat 3, 44, The Covert, Newcastle **To Hold** unto the tenant from the 4th day of January 1988 for a term of 99 years **Yielding and Paying** thereafter during the said term the yearly rent of £160 by equal quarterly payments in advance on the usual quarter days the first of such payments being due proportion thereof to be made on the date hereof for the period to 25th day of March next.

After this are several schedules which detail the covenants entered by the parties, give a detailed description of the flat, list the rights given to the tenant and those rights retained for the landlord and other flat owners (for example rights of support, access, repair and other rights).

a guided tour of the lease

The formal parts of a lease are:

○ premises
○ habendum
○ reddendum
○ covenants
○ provisos
○ options.

Each part has a function to perform.

the premises

This part of the lease includes details of:

the parties to the lease: the names and addresses of the parties and a short description of their respective roles ('landlord' and 'tenant' or 'lessor' and 'lessee');

the date on which the tenancy starts: the commencement date of the term may be earlier, later or at the same time as the date of the deed;

the price paid for the lease is stated as is the ground rent payable. The expression 'Yielding & Paying' used in the lease signifies that the tenant must seek out the landlord to ensure that the ground rent is paid;

the intention of the parties to create a lease: there is no set formula, the more popular expressions used are 'demise', 'lease', 'let', and 'grant and demise' – they all mean the same thing. Any phrase which shows the necessary intention will suffice;

a brief description of the property: this is known as the 'parcels' clause and defines what property is being leased. For a lease of a house, the parcels are usually very straightforward and the address only is required. If the lease is of a flat, the precise boundaries of the flat should be stated: this needs the mention of which walls, floors and ceilings are to be included. A scale plan prepared by an architect or surveyor is often attached. The detailed description is often contained in a schedule to the lease and may read something like:

> "All that flat known as Flat 3, 44 The Covert, Newcastle TOGETHER with the ceilings and floors of the said flat and the joists and beams on which the floors are laid but not the joists and beams to which the ceilings are attached unless those joists and beams also support a floor of the said flat AND TOGETHER with all cisterns tanks sewers drains pipes wires ducts and conduits used solely for the purposes of the said flat but no others EXCEPT AND RESERVING from the demise the main structural parts of the building of which the said flat forms part including the roof foundations and external parts thereof but not the glass of the windows or the window frames of the said flat nor the interior faces of such of the external walls as bound the said flat.
> ALL INTERNAL WALLS separating the Premises from any other part of the building shall be party walls and shall be used repaired and maintained as such."

The description states exactly what the buyer is getting and is relevant in connection with the tenant's repairing obligations. Uncertainty about boundaries would cause problems. Where the lease does not say anything specific about boundaries, there are certain rules of thumb: for example, that the lease of the top flat will carry with it the airspace and roof space above it; that the tenant acquires the space between his floor and the underside of the floor of the flat above; and where the flat has an outside wall the tenant has both sides of the wall.

'except and reserving'

Where the landlord wants to exclude some part of the building from the lease (stairways and passages, for example) or reserve a right of way over some of the premises leased (a garden or pathway, for example), such exceptions and reservations are contained in a further schedule in the lease, for example

> "All those gardens drives paths and forecourts and the halls staircases landings and other parts of the building which are used in common by the owners or occupiers of any two or more of the flats . . . All those main structural parts of the building including 'roof foundations and external parts thereof . . . cisterns tanks sewers drains pipes [etc] not used solely for the purpose of one flat."

various rights

The lease may also grant to each flat owner various rights ('easements') over other flat owners' property in the remainder of the block: rights of access, support and entry for the purpose of carrying out repairs, for example. Correspondingly, the lease will give similar rights over the property leased, for the benefit of other flat owners. But because there is no contractual relationship between the flat owners themselves, these rights can be enforced only via the landlord and not by the other tenants. These rights are often set out in separate schedules within the lease along the following lines:

"Rights included in the demise
1) The right in common with the lessor and occupiers of other flats and all others having the like right to use for purposes only of access to and egress from the premises all such parts of the reserved property as afford access thereto.
2) The right of passage and running of gas electricity water and soil from and to the premises through the sewers drains pipes wires ducts and conduits forming part of the reserved property.
3) The benefit of any covenants entered into by the owners of other flats with the landlord so far as such covenants are intended to benefit the premises of the tenant.
4) All rights of support and other easements and all quasi-easements rights and benefits of a similar nature now enjoyed or intended to be enjoyed by the premises.
5) The right to use in common with the owners and occupiers of all other flats and their visitors the gardens drives paths and forecourts forming part of the reserved property.
6) Such rights of access to and entry upon the reserved property and the other flats as are necessary for the proper performance of the tenant's obligations hereunder."

The tenant will also be subject to certain obligations imposed by the lease, for example

"Rights to which the demise is subject
1) All rights of support and other easements and all quasi-easements rights and benefits of a similar nature now enjoyed or intended to be enjoyed by any other part of the building over the premises.
2) Such rights of access to and entry upon the premises by the landlord and the owners of the other flats as are necessary for the proper performance of their obligations hereunder or under covenants relating to other flats and similar to those herein contained.
3) The burden of any covenants entered into by the landlord with the owners of other flats so far as such covenants are intended to bind the premises or the tenant."

the habendum

This part of the lease states the length of the tenancy (in the example, 99 years). The term normally starts at midnight after the commencement date stated (midnight on the 4th/5th January) and will expire at the end of the last day of the period specified (at the end of 4th January 2087). It is necessary that the beginning of the term is set out with certainty and that its end is specified or can be calculated.

the reddendum

This states what rent the landlord shall be paid. With a long lease of residential property, this is normally ground rent only. Ground rent is a rent for the 'bare-site' of the land (£160 in the example lease) and is substantially lower than the full market rent for the premises. The ground rent is additional to the purchase price of the lease (in the example £50,000) and is usually payable on each 'quarter day' (March 25, June 24, September 29 and December 25). The rent days are specified in the reddendum and the amount will be stated exactly and the dates for payment specified.

the covenants

The covenants form a vital part of the lease and they spell out the liabilities of the parties. They will be considered again in later chapters. Covenants which are commonly found in leases include:

covenants by the tenant
to pay the ground rent, for example

> "The tenant shall pay the reserved rent on the days and in the manner above specified."

to pay rates, for example

"The tenant shall pay all existing and future rates taxes
assessments and outgoings whether parliamentary local or
otherwise now or hereafter imposed or charged upon the
premises or any part thereof or upon the landlord or any
owner or occupier in respect thereof."

to repair, for example

"The tenant shall to the satisfaction in all respects of the
landlord keep the premises and all parts thereof and all
fixtures and fittings therein and all additions thereto in a good
and tenantable state of repair decoration and condition
throughout the continuance of the lease including the renewal
and replacement of all worn or damaged parts and shall
maintain and uphold and whenever necessary for whatever
reason rebuild reconstruct and replace the same and shall
yield up the same at the determination of the lease in such
good and tenantable state of repair decoration and condition
and in accordance with the terms of this covenant in all
respects."

not to make alterations without the landlord's consent, for example

"The tenant shall not make any alterations in the premises
without the approval in writing of the landlord to the plans
and specifications and shall make those alterations only in
accordance with those plans and specifications when
approved."

to insure the property, for example

"Insure and keep insured the Premises against loss or damage
by fire [*and other perils*] in the full value thereof in the names of
the landlord and the tenant through such agency as the
landlord shall from time to time specify with the office of the
Bridstow Insurance Co or with other such insurance office as
the landlord shall from time to time determine and whenever
required produce to the landlord the policy or policies of such
insurance and the receipt for the last premium for the same
and in the event of the premises being damaged or destroyed

by fire or other insured risk as soon as reasonably practicable lay out the insurance moneys in the repair rebuilding or reinstatement of the premises."

not to assign, underlet or part with possession without the consent of the landlord, for example

"The tenant shall not assign or underlet the premises without the previous written consent of the landlord such consent not to be unreasonably withheld."

to use as a private residence only, for example

"The tenant shall not use the premises for any purpose other than as a residence."

to permit the landlord to enter and view the state of the property, for example

"The tenant shall permit the landlord to have access to and enter upon the premises as often as it may be reasonably necessary for him to do so in fulfilment of his obligations hereunder or under covenants relating to other flats and similar to those herein contained."

to pay the service charge
(this will usually be a complicated schedule in the lease; the subject is dealt with later in this book)

to leave the premises on the end of the lease, for example

"That the tenant will at the expiration or sooner determination of the term hereby granted surrender and deliver up to the landlord or his successors in title peaceable and quiet possession of the demised premises."

covenants by the landlord
to allow the tenant the peaceful enjoyment of the premises, for example

"The landlord covenants with the tenant that the tenant shall have quiet enjoyment of the property as against the landlord and all persons claiming through the landlord."

to repair and decorate the outside of the premises, for example

> "The landlord shall keep the reserved property and all fixtures and fittings therein and additions thereto in a good and tenantable state of repair decoration and condition including the renewal and replacement of all worn or damaged parts."

to maintain common parts of the building (lifts, stairways and passages, for instance), for example

> "The landlord shall keep the halls stairs landings and passages forming part of the reserved property properly carpeted cleaned and in good order and shall keep adequately lighted all such parts of the reserved property as are normally lighted or as should be lighted."

the provisos and options

This part of the lease contains the administrative provisions which help towards the smoother running of the relationship between lessor and lessee. The most common proviso gives the landlord the right to terminate the lease if the tenant fails to observe any of the covenants. This is known as a 'forfeiture clause' (forfeiture is considered later in this book).

A forfeiture clause will read something like:

> "PROVIDED ALWAYS and it is hereby agreed that if the rents hereby reserved or any part thereof shall be unpaid for twenty one days after becoming payable (whether formally demanded or not) or if any covenant on the part of the tenant herein contained shall not be performed or observed then and in any such case it shall be lawful for the landlord at any time thereafter to re-enter upon the demised premises or any part thereof in the name of the whole and thereupon this demise shall absolutely determine but without prejudice to any right or action or remedy of the landlord in respect of any antecedent breach of any of the tenant's covenants."

In the lease there may be an option to purchase the freehold (the landlord's reversion), or a right of pre-emption which gives the tenant the right of first refusal if the landlord wishes to sell the freehold. Both can be made available for a specified tenant or extend to subsequent tenants, may exist for a limited time or throughout the lease and may be at a fixed price or at a price to be determined. (All this is considered in a separate chapter.)

assignments, underleases and sale of the landlord's reversion

When an existing lease is assigned, the assignor (the tenant) sells the whole of his interest in the flat. It is similar to creating a new lease but instead of starting "The lease made . . ." it will begin: "The assignment made . . .".

There is normally an account of the grant of the original lease: the date, the parties, the term, the rent and the property. This shows how the present seller came to own the lease. Where the original lease contains a covenant against assignment without the lessor's consent, the assignment will state that the consent has been duly obtained.

The operative part of the deed will be something like:

> ". . . the seller as beneficial owner **Hereby Assigns** unto the buyer **ALL THAT** property described in the schedule hereto and comprised in and demised by the Lease **To Hold** unto the buyer for all the residue now unexpired of the term of years created by the lease **subject** henceforth to the rent reserved by and to the lessee's covenants and conditions contained in the lease."

The property is usually identified in the schedule by reference to the original lease.

> "The property is more fully described in a lease dated 4 January 1988 and made between Desmond Jackson and Mary Rogers."

Normally no new covenants are introduced: the assignee is bound automatically by the existing covenants, on a 'take it or leave it' basis. The assignor remains liable for the fulfilment of existing covenants and therefore an indemnity covenant is implied (that means it does not have to be spelled out in the assignment) that the assignee will reimburse the seller for any non-payment of rent or breach of the other covenants and conditions. There is also an implied covenant that the seller has complied with the terms of the lease.

the grant of an underlease

The grant of a sublease (an underlease and a sublease are the same thing) is not an assignment of the tenant's whole interest in the property. Underleases of residential property are common in the case of new housing estates in some parts of the country. In such estates, the freeholder leases the land to the developer for, say, 999 years at an annual rent of, say, £500. On the land the developer builds 5 blocks of flats, for example, and subleases each individual flat for a term of, say, 990 years at a premium (the purchase price) plus a ground rent of £20 per year. This practice is known as a 'building' or 'letting' scheme.

The conveyance is similar to the grant of a lease, as described earlier. It is important to ensure that the sublease imposes an obligation to observe covenants at least as onerous as those contained in the freeholder's lease. In order to achieve this, the sublease normally states verbatim the relevant covenants appearing in the headlease or incorporates them by reference.

An underlease also includes an indemnity covenant. This is not implied by law and must, therefore, be expressly stated. This would read along these lines:

> "by way of indemnity only to perform and observe such covenants and restrictions contained in the head lease as are still effective and relate to the property and to indemnify the sublessor against any liability resulting from their breach or non-observance."

what happens if the freeholder sells

If the landlord sells his reversionary interest at some stage, the buyer of the reversion acquires the freehold title subject to the existing lease(s). The deed will normally read:

> "**To Hold** unto the purchaser in fee simple subject to but with the benefit of the before recited lease."

that means that the buyer of the freehold reversion can enforce the tenant's covenants contained in the lease; similarly, the buyer of the freehold will be bound by the landlord's covenants contained in the existing lease.

When it is the existing tenant who buys the reversion, a term that the lease will merge with and be extinguished by the freehold will generally be incorporated into the conveyance. (A specimen of this term is shown on page 170). This will avoid questions being raised when the property is sold subsequently.

All tenants have right to be informed if the landlord has sold his freehold reversion and must be told the name and address of the new owners.

LANDLORD
owns freehold (reversion)
and can sell it if he wishes.
Whoever owns the free-
hold at the end of the
tenant's lease will get back
the property (flat)

lease

sale

BUYER OF REVERSION
becomes freeholder of
property and the new landlord of the flat-owner (tenant); takes on all rights and
duties of original landlord

TENANT
on being granted lease
acquires the right of occupation and the legal ownership of the flat for the term
of the lease (eg 99 years);
can sell (assign) the lease
or create (grant) a shorter
one (underlease or sub-
lease)

assignment

sublease

SUBTENANT
buys a fixed term lease
shorter (eg 10 years) than
the original tenant's
remaining term; original
tenant becomes landlord of
subtenant and gets back
the flat at the end of the
sublease (on expiry of the
10 years). The subtenant
can sell (assign) his sublease, if he wishes, or sub-
sublet for a shorter term
(eg 8 years)

ASSIGNEE
buys the unexpired term of
the original lease (eg 90
years) and takes on all
rights and duties of the
original tenant; can sell
(assign) the remainder of
the lease or sublet the flat if
he wishes

THE COMPLEX CHAIN OF LIABILITY

Most flat buyers appreciate that they are acquiring a temporary ownership of the property during the continuance of the lease. It is also generally understood that the lease represents a contract between the original tenant and the original landlord and that the terms of the lease and the covenants must be complied with. Normally, the covenants remain enforceable throughout the existence of the lease. The consequences of this are often greater than people may imagine.

effect of assignment

When a tenant assigns the lease (that is, the current owner of the flat sells it to a new one), the assignee (buyer) becomes automatically liable to the landlord with regard to the tenant's covenants. The assignee remains liable for as long as he has the lease. If he assigns it to someone else, this liability ceases.

The original tenant (the 'assignor') will remain liable on the covenants during the subsistence of the lease.

Similarly, when the original landlord parts with the freehold, the successor is responsible for complying with the landlord's covenants. Again, this liability continues while he remains the freeholder.

The original landlord, however, also remains liable on the covenants.

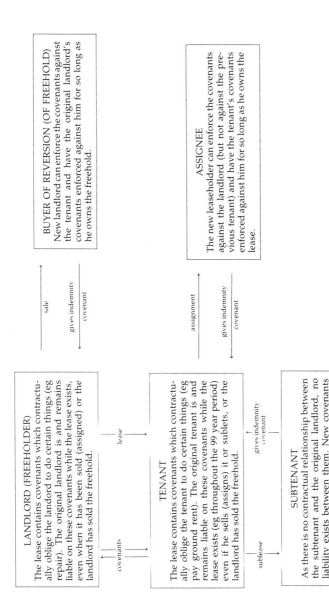

LANDLORD (FREEHOLDER)
The lease contains covenants which contractually oblige the landlord to do certain things (eg repair). The original landlord is and remains liable on these covenants while the lease exists, even when it has been sold (assigned) or the landlord has sold the freehold.

BUYER OF REVERSION (OF FREEHOLD)
New landlord can enforce the covenants against the tenant and have the original landlord's covenants enforced against him for so long as he owns the freehold.

sale
gives indemnity covenant

TENANT
The lease contains covenants which contractually oblige the tenant to do certain things (eg pay ground rent). The original tenant is and remains liable on these covenants while the lease exists (eg throughout the 99 year period) even if he sells (assigns) it or sublets, or the landlord has sold the freehold.

ASSIGNEE
The new leaseholder can enforce the covenants against the landlord (but not against the previous tenant) and have the tenant's covenants enforced against him for so long as he owns the lease.

assignment
gives indemnity covenant

lease
covenants

SUBTENANT
As there is no contractual relationship between the subtenant and the original landlord, no liability exists between them. New covenants between grantor of sublease and subtenant will echo those between original freeholder and original tenant because they both remain liable.

sublease
gives indemnity covenant

Because liability remains, each assignor adds a covenant to be indemnified if new owner breaches any existing covenants.

effect of subletting
Where the original tenant does not wish to dispose of the flat outright and, as an alternative, sublets the property, he will pass on the obligations to the subtenant in the sublease. But it is the tenant who remains fully liable to the original landlord, because there is clearly no contract between the landlord and the subtenant. The tenant will therefore expressly make the subtenant liable to indemnify him, the tenant, for any claims made by the landlord arising from breaches by the subtenant.

the trap

A person who takes a long lease of residential property does not expect to have anything more to do with the flat after selling it to someone else. But the original tenant continues to have responsibility to ensure that the obligations undertaken in the lease are fulfilled and this is so even after parting with the flat.

As shown, the assignee of the lease has direct liability to the landlord, but the covenants may still continue to be enforced against the original tenant. It is usual for the landlord to look to the assignee first. There is, however, nothing to prevent redress being sought against the original tenant immediately.

Accordingly, the original tenant can be liable for someone else's default, many years after parting with the flat. Such a claim would come as a shock and likely to be beyond his means.

By way of an example, imagine the situation where the original tenant had substantial repair covenants in a lease which has subsequently been assigned several times. The present assignee is in breach of the repair covenants contained in his assignment and has no money to finance the work required. The lease now has less than 40 years to run and, even if the property were in good repair, it might be difficult to sell. The landlord can sue the present assignee for compensation, but there is little point in suing someone who does not have the funds to pay. The landlord may seek to forfeit the lease, but the court will usually allow the tenant to stay on. The landlord may have no other effective remedy except as against the original tenant. The original tenant will be liable for breach of covenant and will not be able to take practical advantage of the express or implied indemnity covenant because the assignee has no funds from which to reimburse the original tenant.

Landlords are in a similar predicament. Where the original landlord parts with the freehold, the liability remains to perform the obligations expressed in the lease.

indemnity

If the original tenant or landlord becomes liable to pay damages because of an assignee's breach of covenant, the original party can seek reimbursement because of two types of indemnity (but the effectiveness depends on the solvency of the assignee).

implied
The original tenant has an implied legal right of reimbursement against the assignee currently in possession of the flat. An indemnity covenant will be implied into an assignment. Under this covenant, the assignee agrees to indemnify the assignor against all future claims for payments of rent and to observe and perform the obligations imposed by the lease.

A similar principle applies between the original landlord and the current owner of the freehold.

expressed

In almost every assignment, there is, however, an express covenant to indemnify the original tenant against such claims. On subsequent assignments a similar covenant will be expressly incorporated and it is, therefore, common for a chain of indemnities to exist.

Although the successors in title of the landlord become liable on the landlord's covenants, there is no implied covenant to indemnify. The original landlord would, therefore, be wise to insert an express provision as to reimbursement into a contract for the sale of the freehold.

There is no implied indemnity between subtenant and his landlord. An indemnity covenant should therefore be included in the sublease.

WHEN THE PROFESSIONAL GETS IT WRONG

Going to law is a risky, time-consuming and potentially expensive adventure. In many situations, however, it is a worthwhile and necessary enterprise. As the purchase of somewhere to live constitutes the major investment in many people's lives, when things go wrong it can be a financially ruinous experience.

Professionals become involved at various stages of the process of buying and selling a home. The price to be paid is worked out by a valuer; the structural soundness and state of the property is assessed by a surveyor; the title to the property is checked and later conveyed by a solicitor or licensed conveyancer.

There may be defects in the design or construction of the building or conversion work which may be due to the fault of an architect or builder, for example.

When the professional gets it wrong, the possible avenues for legal action are for a breach of contract and/or negligence. A breach of contract action has generally to be started within 6 years of the date of the contract. Liability for contractual breach is, however, severely limited by a concept known as 'privity'. The essence of this legal notion is that only a party to the contract can sue or be sued under its terms. It is highly likely that those who suffer loss because of the fault of a valuer, surveyor, architect will not be privy to any contract with that professional because he was employed by a third party with whom he had a contract. This is when the law of negligence comes into its own.

negligence

Negligence is a wide and ever expanding area of the law. Claims which are based on the negligence of the professionally-qualified have become more frequent than those for breach of contract in a similar situation. The law has developed extensively in order to protect the rights of the consumer, but getting compensation is not always a straightforward matter.

Negligence concerns the liability for injury and loss caused by someone's fault. The essence of the law is that reasonable care has to be taken so as not to injure anyone reasonably foreseeable as being affected by one's acts. This has become known as the 'neighbour principle'. It covers persons who have no contractual relationship with the professional.

the three ingredients

It is necessary that certain factors be established before an action in negligence can be successful.

A duty of care must exist, recognised by the law and owed directly to the injured party. Most claims will fall within this scope, and anyone who is a reasonably foreseeable victim will be protected.

Surveyors, architects and the like will owe a duty of care to, for example, the original landlord and tenant, subsequent assignees and subtenants. It matters not that there was no contract with the professional.

There must be a breach of that duty. It is not for every mistake or careless act that a person will be liable in negligence. The person at fault must fall short of an objective standard set by the courts before liability will be imposed. The yardstick which is used is that of 'the reasonable man'. As regards professional liability, the standard of care is that of the reasonably competent person of that particular calling (architect or solicitor, for example).

The standard varies according to what skills are professed and expected. The problem is that it is not always clear what the average professional should have done. It is not certain, for example, when a solicitor will have been negligent in the conveyancing process. Should the solicitor make a physical inspection of the property to discover whether anyone other than the seller lives there? Should the buyer's solicitor be content with relying on evasive replies of the seller's solicitor to the preliminary enquiries and requisitions? The answer to such questions is not definite and would have to be worked out by the court in all the circumstances of the case. This may to a large extent depend on the practice adopted by a significant part of the profession.

The law does not expect professionals to be infallible. Not every error will give rise to liability. A valuer is not automatically liable to compensate a seller or a buyer or a mortgagee for any loss caused by any under- or over-valuation. The mistake must be viewed against the general standard of care applicable to that particular expertise. In the case of the valuer, a very general rule has emerged that a 15% inaccuracy in valuation is permissible.

There must be damage arising from the breach of duty and this damage must be a reasonably foreseeable consequence. The law, therefore, only imposes liability where the loss would not have occurred 'but for' the fault and sets an arbitrary line beyond which compensation cannot be claimed.

influential factors

In deciding whether a professional is liable in negligence, some factors may assume a crucial importance.

The court will look at what the professional was instructed to do. A surveyor, for example, may be commissioned to undertake surveys which differ in the depth of the investigation to be carried out and the cost of the exercise. It may be that a defect that should have been discovered on the most thorough (and expensive) survey does not appear on the basic (and cheaper) investigation. Where the surveyor has been instructed to carry out a less detailed survey, liability will not arise for failing to note a defect which would only have been discoverable on a more extensive survey.

The professional is expected to keep up-to-date with the law and practice relating to that profession. An architect, for example, has to keep abreast of developments in design, roofing and heating matters. A failure to do so could result in a successful claim for negligence.

Similarly, the professional is required to avoid well-known or recognised hazards of the work to be carried out. A solicitor, for example, should (in theory) always inspect the property to be bought in order to find out whether a person other than the seller is living there and has any rights over the property. The solicitor who omits to do this could be liable in negligence.

The court will place much emphasis upon the customs and codes of practice of the particular profession. A departure from such custom and professional guidance may indicate a breach of the duty to take care. The relevant time for assessing this is when the negligence is alleged to have occurred, and not years later when the matter reaches the court and standards may have changed.

problem areas:

There are several areas of the law of negligence and also of contract which, in certain circumstances, may limit liability or prevent it arising.

exclusion clauses

It is possible that the professional will attempt to disclaim responsibility by inserting into a contract or report, for example, a statement excluding liability. (This is not, however, common practice because it is not good for business and reflects poorly on the standards of that profession.) If such a clause is inserted, it is ineffective as regards liability for physical injury caused and, in relation to damage to property, as a general rule effective only if it is reasonable.

Another similar way in which a surveyor could protect himself is by couching a report in vague terms, for example, 'it is possible that . . .' 'not to our observations' or 'it may be that . . .'. Where the surveyor is not making a positive statement on which the buyer can rely and merely hedging his bets by alerting the buyer to possibilities, it would be difficult to bring a successful claim.

time limits

In most areas of the law, proceedings need to be started within set time limits. So, for example, the limitation period for breach of contract is, generally, 6 years and, in the case of negligence, 3 years for personal injury matters and 6 years for other claims.

Of particular relevance to property owners, however, is the Latent Defects Act 1986. This Act tackles the problem of when time begins to run. As a general rule, time begins to run from the date of the negligent act, but in some cases the damage does not arise until much later. In the case of negligent construction, for example, there may be difficulty in ascertaining when time starts to run: the date when the damage first appears? or when the plaintiff (the person bringing the action) acquires the flat? or the date when the plaintiff first discovers the damage? The Act is of particular use in this area and provides that:

○ as regards latent damage not involving personal injury, the relevant period is either 6 years from the negligent act or 3 years from the date on which the plaintiff knew, or ought to have known, of the damage, whichever is the later. There is, however, a ceiling of 15 years from the date of the negligence beyond which the action will be out of time;
○ where the building is acquired by successive owners, a fresh right of action arises and time starts to run from the date when the property is bought;
○ similar time limits apply also to where the plaintiff suffers financial loss by relying on carelessly given professional advice.

negligent advice

Liability can arise from negligent statements being made. For a duty of care to arise it is necessary that a 'special relationship' exists between the parties. The ingredients of this special relationship are that:

○ it must be reasonable to consult the professional for the advice; and

○ the professional must know (or should know) that the advice is to be relied upon; and

○ it is reasonable to rely on that advice.

However, it is not necessary for the plaintiff to have paid for the advice.

A solicitor or valuer, for example, will be liable for negligently giving advice which causes economic loss to the client and any other person who could be reasonably anticipated as being affected.

Where an adviser uses the phrase 'without responsibility' (or a similar statement), he would be avoiding liability.

economic loss

Pure economic loss (that is loss which is unassociated with physical injury or damage to property) is, as a general rule, irrecoverable. The major exception to this concerns negligent advice: the plaintiff can recover for pure economic loss which arises from a negligent misstatement. As most claims involving the purchase of a flat, and work undertaken on the premises, will involve damage to the building or be based on negligent advice, this restriction will rarely be a bar to getting compensation.

Defective Premises Act 1972

At common law, the builder of a house was under certain limited contractual obligations to the person who engaged him (and with whom he had a contract): first, that the work shall be done in a good and workmanlike manner; second, that good and proper materials will be used; and, third, that the house will be reasonably fit for human habitation. Apart from this implied form of warranty, the general rule was 'let the buyer beware'.

The law of negligence has gradually extended its scope to make builders, architects and surveyors, for example, liable for their failures to take reasonable care. In addition, certain duties are imposed under the Defective Premises Act 1972.

The Act is relevant here on two fronts: first, it creates a statutory duty to build dwellings properly and, second, it abolishes the 'buyer beware' rule.

duty to build properly

A person who takes on work connected with the construction, conversion or extension of a building owes a duty of care not only to the person who commissions the work but, importantly, to subsequent buyers of the dwelling. The duty is to see that the work is done in a professional manner, with proper materials and so as to ensure that the premises are fit for habitation.

The duty is imposed on builders, architects, surveyors and local authorities, for example, and cannot be excluded or restricted by any agreement. Any action must be brought within 6 years of the building work being completed.

liability of sellers

The Act abolishes the seller's immunity from liability in negligence. So, where the seller has undertaken work of construction, repair, maintenance or demolition or any other work connected to the premises, there is a duty of care owed to subsequent buyers.

if the case goes to court

Legal aid may be available to either party in a civil court action for negligence or breach of contract.

The grant of legal aid depends on the financial status of the claimant and also on the merits of the case: the yardstick is whether a reasonable person would be advised to go to court at the risk of incurring costs.

The proceedings will be heard in the county court if the claim is for less than £5000 and the High Court for claims above this sum. The process will take approximately 2 to 3 years in the county court and often longer in the High Court. Not surprisingly, therefore, legal costs are often staggeringly high. It is crucial, therefore, that the other (the loser) pays the costs of the action.

MORE ABOUT COVENANTS

The covenants in a lease usually state the rights and the obligations of the parties to it.

Covenants may be positive in nature (that is, they compel a party to do something: for example, to repair or to insure) or negative (that is, they restrict a party from doing something: for example, not using the premises for business purposes or assigning the lease without consent). Positive covenants bind the original landlord and tenant and any buyers from them. Such covenants affect successors in title even though they were not parties to the original contract.

Both parties normally enter into a series of express covenants. In the majority of cases, the rights and liabilities of the parties are fixed by express terms, namely the covenants actually spelled out in the lease. Examples of covenants frequently found in a long lease are illustrated earlier in this book. Usually the heavier burden is placed on the tenant.

For express covenants, the exact wording used can be crucial. Much turns on the precise draftmanship by the solicitors involved. The importance of the words used will be illustrated in the context of repairing covenants, but is equally relevant in all the covenants.

Covenants may also be referred to by implication (a reference in the lease to the 'usual' covenants) or implied by law. ('Implied' means: not written in but nevertheless present.)

their purpose

The comfort and enjoyment of living in a flat or maisonette (and also its resale value) often depend on the state of maintenance and repair of the remainder of the building, the extent and quality of the services provided (such as lifts, heating and cleaning of common parts) and the upkeep of amenities (gardens and access roads). Appropriate covenants are therefore included in the lease and are enforceable by the landlord against each tenant and by each tenant against the landlord.

Generally, as no contract exists between the tenants themselves, one tenant cannot sue another when a covenant has been breached. A statutory exception to this rule is where a covenant imposed by the landlord expressly benefits other tenants. This covenant would read:

> "The Tenant **HEREBY COVENANTS** with the Landlord and with the tenants of other flats comprised in the Building that the Tenant will at all times hereafter [*then a list of the obligations*]."

The covenants that go into the lease when it is created can be the subject of negotiation between the tenant and the landlord. Once in the lease, the general rule is that they remain unchangeable. (The Landlord and Tenant Act 1987 does, however, give the county court the power to alter terms if necessary. This is dealt with later in the book.)

When an existing lease is assigned, the covenants contained in it will apply between the asssignor and the assignee. The assignor can introduce new covenants if that is desirable, but generally will insert only an indemnity covenant.

basic legal principles

Both the original landlord and the tenant remain liable on the covenants for the duration of the lease even when either party has sold his interest under the lease. The original covenantors will remain liable for breaches caused by subsequent buyers and an indemnity covenant is therefore usually inserted into subsequent sales of both the landlord's and the tenant's interests. This right to indemnity is also implied into the assignment of a lease.

express obligations of the landlord

Commonly found covenants include:

repair

The landlord may enter into a covenant to repair the premises where a block of flats is involved. If there is nothing in the lease about this, the landlord is under no implied obligation to repair and the tenant, when he moves in, must take the premises as found. Nor will the landlord do anything about repairs afterwards.

A repairing obligation may be shared so that the landlord is liable for external repairs and the tenant for internal repairs. It is rare for the landlord to undertake internal repairs. The landlord's work will be paid for out of the service charges paid by the tenants, that means the landlord takes the responsibility for arranging repairs, but they are paid for by the tenants. It may be that the landlord's obligation is limited to certain areas of the building (for example, common parts, roofing and drains).

The landlord can insert an express covenant that he will only be liable if aware of the disrepair. It would then be up to the tenant to bring such matters to the notice of the landlord.

The landlord who is under a repairing obligation may expressly have the right to enter the premises in order to look at the state of repair and to carry out the necessary work. The relevant phrase in the lease would read

> "That the Landlord and his agents surveyors or workmen may at all reasonable times during the said Lease enter upon any part of the demised premises and inspect the state and condition thereof."

insurance

The landlord may have the right to insure the premises or specify a named insurer which the tenant has to use. The covenant may allow the landlord to take out an insurance policy and require the tenant to pay the premiums by way of an addition to ground rent.

An express obligation may require that any insurance settlement is to be spent on reinstating the premises.

peaceful occupation

The landlord may write into the lease an express covenant for 'quiet enjoyment'. Quiet enjoyment is the guarantee that the tenant remains free of any physical interference with, or interruption of, the enjoyment of living in the premises. The covenant has little to do with noise and decibels. It ensures that the landlord does not disturb the tenant's occupation either legally or physically. More than an interference with the comfort of the tenant would be necessary for a breach of this covenant to arise.

A breach will, however, occur if the landlord harasses the tenant or attempts unlawfully to terminate the lease.

This covenant is implied into all leases even where it is not written in as an express obligation.

express obligations of the tenant

Some commonly found covenants include the following.

to pay ground rent and service charges

It is necessary to state to whom the ground rent and service charge is payable and the exact amount of the rent and how the service charges are calculated.

not to assign or sublet

In a residential lease, there is rarely an absolute prohibition but the covenant normally requires the consent of the landlord before any assignment or subletting. This consent must not be unreasonably withheld.

not to make improvements or alterations

There may be an express provision in the lease and this may be absolute or subject to the landlord's consent. If consent is required, it cannot be unreasonably withheld. An example of this covenant is:

"Not to make any alterations or additions to the structure of the demised premises or the plan or the layout thereof or remove any of the landlord's fixtures and fittings without the previous consent in writing of the Landlord."

The landlord may also require that the tenant must pay a reasonable sum to compensate for any decrease in the value of the premises. There may be a covenant that the tenant undertakes to reinstate the premises to their original condition if the improvement does not add to the value of the premises (the converse does not, however, apply: if it adds to the value, the landlord will not compensate the tenant). The undertaking might read:

"to maintain and keep in good order condition and repair the Premises demised and at the expiration or sooner determination of the Lease deliver up to the Landlord the premises in such good and substantial repair order and condition·"

to restrict the use of the premises

The landlord may, for example, restrict the use of the property for residential purposes only by including an appropriate covenant.

An additional express covenant will be that the tenant must not do, or permit to be done, on the premises anything which may become a nuisance or annoyance to other occupiers or the landlord. This might read:

"That no act matter or thing which shall or may be or become or grow to be a public or private nuisance or a damage annoyance grievance or inconvenience to the Landlord or any occupier of adjoining neighbouring or other land or buildings or which may lessen the value of any such land or buildings shall be made carried on or done or suffered on the demised premises."

There may be specific prohibitions: no musical instruments to be played after 10 pm; no washing to be hung outside; no pets except dogs and cats – or no pets at all. Sometimes there is a whole schedule of regulations about use and behaviour with which the tenant must comply.

insurance

The tenant may have to insure the premises for fire and other damage and the covenant may require the tenant to use a named company or one approved by the landlord (it is, however, more usual for the landlord to insure the building and the tenant to pay the premiums).

repairs

Various expressions are used to describe the extent of the obligation imposed on the tenant by a covenant to repair the premises. Typical examples include: 'good tenantable repair', 'good and tenantable order and repair', 'well and substantial repair' and 'perfect repair'. By the choice of language used, the standard of repair is set as high or as low as the parties wish, especially the landlord. But the expressions given above add little to the burden imposed by the basic term 'repair'.

Under a typical long lease the repairing covenants entered into by the tenant are:

○ to keep the premises in good repair: this will usually only relate to internal repairs – the landlord is usually liable for structural and external matters, but in a small block, the covenant may stipulate good repair both internally and externally;

○ to do specific works of repair or maintenance at stated

intervals: for example, to paint inside once every 7 years and outside once every 3 years;
○ to deliver up the premises in good repair at the end of the tenancy or to pay a required sum if they are not.

It is important to appreciate the extent of the obligation to repair. The liability of the tenant may be formidable. If, as a last resort, the landlord were to take legal action against the tenant, the approach of the courts is to look at the particular building, the state which it was in at the start of the lease as far as this can be ascertained, and the precise wording of the covenant. The standard against which the state of repairs is measured is the condition in which the premises would be kept by a reasonably minded owner.

If the premises are in a state of disrepair at the beginning of the lease, a covenant by the tenant to 'put' or 'keep' them in repair imposes an obligation to put them in the required state within a reasonable time. In other cases, however, there is no requirement to make good any defects in the property existing when the lease is granted: that would be an obligation to improve and not merely repair. The tenant is not required to improve the premises.

The repair covenant may except 'fair wear and tear' damage (that is disrepair caused by ordinary natural causes). This does not mean, however, that the tenant can stand by idly and watch the ravages of time take their course. The tenant will be expected to prevent further damage arising.

There may be a covenant that the premises shall be in good repair at the end of the lease. At the end of a long lease, the premises need not be in the same condition as when they were originally leased. Accepting that the age of the premises will show, the property need only be maintained in a condition in keeping with that type of property with reference to its character and locality.

'the usual covenants'

A lease may instead of containing a long list of covenants expressly be made subject to the 'usual' covenants without containing any details as to what these covenants are. This is rare in a long lease.

The 'usual covenants' include:

○ covenant by the tenant to pay rent and rates;
○ covenant by the tenant to keep and deliver up the premises in repair and allow the landlord to enter and view the state of repair;
○ covenant by the landlord for quiet enjoyment;
○ a proviso for re-entry, that means, the landlord can take steps to take possession of the flat on the non-payment of rent or breach of other covenant.

What other covenants are to be included in the description of 'the usual' depends on the nature of the premises, their location and the purpose for which they are being let. It might take legal action before the court to find out what covenants are 'usual' in the circumstances.

implied obligations

When the lease says nothing about them, certain obligations are traditionally implied.

of the landlord:

○ a covenant for quiet enjoyment;
○ a covenant against derogation from grant.

What this means is that the landlord may not seek to take away with one hand what is given with the other. To constitute a derogation from grant there would have to be some act which renders the premises substantially less fit for the purposes for which they were let. Excessive noise and interference with the light which reaches the windows of the tenant have been held to be breaches of this covenant.

There is, however, no covenant that the property is suitable for the tenant's needs.

of the tenant:

○ a covenant not to cause 'waste'.

'Waste' is defined as any action or inaction which alters the physical character of the premises and may be voluntary or permissive waste. Voluntary waste includes any positive acts which diminish the value of the property. Permissive waste covers failures of maintenance and repair, leading to dilapidation of the premises. Because of the implied obligation, if there is no express provision for repair, the tenant is still required to undertake basic repair and maintenance of the premises.

If the landlord is under an obligation to repair, the tenant impliedly covenants to allow the landlord to enter and view the property.

○ There is implied a covenant by the tenant not to do anything which could prejudice the landlord's title, such as, for example, assisting a third party to challenge the landlord's title to the property.

JOINT VENTURES AND MISADVENTURES

English law is not renowned for its simplicity. The recognition and enforcement of the property rights of individuals living together is a complicated matter, but a vital area for many home buyers.

buying a flat together

It is commonplace for a flat to be bought jointly with a spouse or relative(s) or other friend(s). It is advisable in order to avoid complications when the time comes to sell the flat, or if the co-owners fall out with each other, that the names of both the buyers (all of them, if more than two) appear on the conveyancing documents and the lease.

There are two recognised and distinct types of co-ownership: the so-called joint tenancy and the tenancy in common.

Where there is a joint tenancy, the co-owners own all of the property together and on the death of one, the other automatically acquires the property, regardless of any will or the rules which apply on dying intestate (that is, without a will).

Where there is a tenancy in common, each co-owner has a share of the property with which – theoretically – they can do as they please. The partners may own the property half-and-half or in any proportion they wish. On the death of one, the share of the deceased does not automatically go to the other tenant but passes under a will or the intestacy rules.

It is for the buyers to decide which type of arrangement is appropriate. It often depends on the personal relationship between them and the amount of the financial contributions each has made to the purchase. Unless the contrary is expressed, it is presumed that, where unequal contributions are made, the parties intended to create a tenancy in common. Here are some examples.

the married couple:

John and Mary are married and buy a flat together. They both make sure that both their names are on the lease or assignment. By expressly using the phrase 'as joint tenants' and thus creating a joint tenancy, Mary will, on John's death, become automatically the sole owner of the flat, and vice versa.

the unmarried couple:

Desmond and Debbie buy a flat to live in together. It is not their intention that, on the death of one, the other should benefit: both wish to leave their share of the flat to their respective families. They therefore expressly create a tenancy in common by making sure that this phrase is used in the lease or assignment.

unequal contributions

John and Mary are not concerned about the commercial aspect of the transaction. Although Mary has financed only 1/3rd of the purchase price, this does not affect the joint tenancy, and they will own the whole of the flat jointly. If the joint tenancy is severed (that is, ended) the co-owners will have equal shares notwithstanding unequal contributions to the purchase price.

Desmond may feel justified in making sure that Debbie only has a 1/3rd share in the flat (and, thus 1/3 of the proceeds from a subsequent sale). The tenancy in common gives effect to this by saying, in the lease or assignment, that the property is to be held beneficially on trust as tenants in common in proportion of 2/3 to 1/3. If the relationship ends, at least their shares in the flat are clearly defined.

changing relationships

John and Mary are considering a separation or even a divorce. The joint tenancy does not now suit either partner, if only because neither wishes to benefit the other on his or her death. They now seek to sever their joint tenancy and convert it into a tenancy in common. This may be done simply and effectively by giving written notice of the intention to the other party. Following this 'severance' of the joint tenancy, the property is held by them as tenants in common. Were Mary to die, her 50% interest in the flat could be left by will to whomever she pleases. The same applies in the case of John.

Desmond and Debbie get married and want to convert their tenancy in common into a joint tenancy. This can be done by creating a 'trust', in writing. There is no formula or special way of doing so laid down, and a deed is not required. Their names already appear as the legal owners on the lease or assignment.

the co-ownership trust for sale

The law employs a concept known as a 'trust for sale' in every case of co-ownership. This artificial and somewhat confusing notion requires that the co-owners hold the legal ownership (the paper title) on trust for themselves as beneficiaries. Behind this paper title, what really counts is the beneficial enjoyment of the flat and the distinction between the joint tenancy and the tenancy in common assumes its significance.

In this way, the legal and equitable (or beneficial) ownerships are kept apart and the administration of the property is separated from the enjoyment of it. The purpose of this legal fiction is to make the procedure for selling the flat easier and to ensure that both beneficiaries – that is, the co-owners – obtain the proper share of the proceeds of the sale.

When the flat is conveyed into more than one name, the trust for sale arises either expressly or impliedly. The lease may, for example, expressly state that Jack and Jill hold the legal estate on a trust for sale for themselves beneficially. If they are tenants in common, the lease would say:

> "The Purchasers agree that they are in equity tenants in common in the following shares: Jack two-thirds and Jill one-third."

If there is no mention of a trust in the lease, it is implied by law. Jill and Jack have an equal right to occupation of the flat and when it is sold have rights to the proceeds of sale of the property in proportion to their share in it – 1/3rd and 2/3rds respectively.

Under the 'trust for sale', the law regards Jack and Jill as being under a duty to sell the flat (which is not what the couple will wish to do: they will have little interest in the immediate sale of their home but will be more preoccupied in retaining the flat as a secure family base). The duty to sell is, however, another fiction because the trustees (Jack and Jill) have the power to postpone sale and, therefore, the flat will be retained until they decide to sell and move elsewhere.

The 'trust for sale' ensures that when the flat is sold, at whatever distant date, the process of transfer to the new buyer is simplified. The buyer will be able to obtain an absolute title without concerning himself with the beneficial interests of Jack and Jill.

when buying from trustees for sale

It is crucial that the buyer acquires the property free from the beneficial interests of the co-owners. This will happen if he:

○ takes a conveyance from the trustees (ie the legal owners as stated on the lease or assignment); and
○ pays the purchase money to at least 2 trustees (in our example, to both Jack and Jill).

The buyer takes a good legal title and is unconcerned with Jack and Jill. Their interests under either the joint tenancy or tenancy in common are transferred into the proceeds of sale – the money they get from selling the flat. The buyer is not liable for any misapplication of the funds if, for example, Jack absconds, having withdrawn the purchase money from a joint bank account.

the decision to sell a co-owned flat

There is no problem when all the co-owners consent to the

sale. The difficulties arise when there is a dispute between the owners themselves. The rule is that the sale cannot go ahead unless the co-owners agree. In circumstances where one co-owner refuses, the other(s) may apply to the court for an order compelling the reluctant party to join in.

The basic law is that there is a duty to sell and a power to postpone the sale. But the court is given a wide discretion 'to make such order as it thinks fit', so it is possible that it would withhold enforcement. In the exercise of its discretion, the court must look into all the circumstances of the case and consider whether it is right and proper that the sale be enforced against the wishes of one of the co-owners. In two situations the court will most likely decide against sale:

formal agreement

The first is where the co-owners have agreed between themselves not to sell the flat without the consent of all. This may be the case where acquaintances buy a flat together and fear that one of them may wish to leave. If the co-owners had formally, in writing, agreed that none of them will sell for a specified period (perhaps 2 years), the court will generally uphold this arrangement.

family home

Where the co-owners bought the property in order to provide a family home, the trust for sale has the purpose of providing a home for joint occupation by the members of a family. The court will be unwilling to allow the property to be sold against the wishes of one co-owner while the need for a family home continues (for example, while dependent children require a roof over their heads).

THE FLAT AS THE MATRIMONIAL HOME

Special considerations arise where one spouse is the sole owner, with the other spouse having no ownership of the matrimonial home. Take Peter and Celia as an example. Peter has bought the flat and it is conveyed into his name. Celia has made no contributions to the purchase of the flat or its running costs. She is not a co-owner. Both the common law and statute offer Celia, a non-owning spouse, some protection from being put out on the street. These rights are binding on the owning spouse and also, in some cases, the buyer of the flat from the spouse. Against a background of increased marital breakdown, these rights have assumed great importance. The law has gone some way towards ensuring residential security for the disadvantaged spouse.

the common law right

It has long been the case that a wife (and, presumably, now a husband) has a right to occupy the matrimonial home and use the furniture in it. This arises simply because of the marriage and the status of being a spouse.

This common law right is binding only on the other spouse and does not affect third parties – that is, for example, a new buyer of the property. In addition, the right extends only to those in a legal marriage and offers no protection to an unmarried partner or other member of the family.

the Matrimonial Homes Act 1983

This Act gives the non-owning spouse a statutory right to occupy the matrimonial home. In practice, it is more far-reaching than the common law.

The right afforded by the 1983 Act is 'the right not to be evicted or excluded from the dwelling house or any part thereof by the other spouse' except when a court order is obtained. If not in occupation (that is, not living there) a spouse has, with the leave of the court, the right to enter into and occupy the premises. The statutory right of occupation lasts throughout the duration of the marriage, but ceases on decree absolute. It can be released, in writing – perhaps while the couple are separating.

The right extends to the flat and any garden, garage, yard or outhouse forming part of the lease, as long as the dwelling had been the spouses' matrimonial home. The spouse has no right to occupy a flat into which the other spouse has moved after their separation and which has never been their matrimonial home.

For as long as a spouse has a right of occupation, either party may apply to the court for an order declaring, enforcing, restricting or terminating the right. The court can make such an order as it considers 'just and equitable' (that is, fair) having regard to the parties' needs and resources, the needs of children and all the circumstances of the case.

the statutory rights and third parties

The Matrimonial Homes Act 1983 provides a scheme of registration by which what are merely personal rights may become transformed into proprietary rights, binding on everyone. A non-owning spouse's right of occupation can be registered as a charge on the property of the other spouse. In themselves, without registration, the rights considered above have no impact on people outside the family unit: if the owning-spouse assigns the lease to a third party or re-mortgages the property, it is probable that the other spouse's rights of occupation would be destroyed.

entry on the register

In the unregistered system of conveyancing, the statutory right may be registered against the name of the owner as a 'class F' land charge. In the case of a registered property, the right may be entered as a notice at the Land Registry. For both, and as a departure from the normal rules, the entry can be unilateral and without the consent and knowledge of the owning-spouse.

A charge or notice can be entered against only one property. It does not matter that the spouse who is registering has ceased to live in the flat.

The consequence of registration is that any future buyers would buy the property subject to the spouse's occupation. The lease will, therefore, be rendered unmarketable. Registration can be used as weapon of hostility and spite: the ease and secrecy by which a charge or notice may be entered can effectively frustrate any proposed assignment of the lease. The tenant could easily be blackmailed by the non-owning spouse into buying off the charge or notice.

The right, however, ceases on divorce, and the registered entry should be cancelled by either of the ex-spouses.

Without registration of the charge or notice, the right of occupation does not bind a subsequent buyer and this is regardless of whether or not the buyer knew of the spouse's rights.

Many spouses are not aware of this form of protection and there is therefore a low take-up of the facility of registration.

the flat as the ex-matrimonial home

Much litigation is focused upon what is to happen to the family home on the breakdown of a marriage. One dilemma which commonly emerges is that one partner wishes to sell and the other wishes to remain in occupation of the flat.

Where the parties are married, the divorce court has the power to make a property adjustment order. This means that, when the divorce or judicial separation order is granted, the court can adjust the property rights between the spouses. In making the order, all the circumstances of the case should be taken into account. Particular attention will be focused on the welfare of any children and also the financial resources and needs of the parties. The direct and indirect contributions of each spouse to the acquisition and/or running of the family home are also of importance.

CO-OWNERSHIP BY IMPLICATION

Where there is co-ownership and the property is conveyed into the name of one party only, even though the money comes from both buyers, the law presumes that the person whose name appears on the documents of title is the only owner of that property. In order to obtain a share in the purchase money when the flat is later sold, the other party must show that an implied trust has been created.

Where the flat is conveyed into one name only, and problems or disputes emerge as to entitlement to future proceeds of sale, the court must determine the intentions of the parties and whether co-ownership exists and calculate the proportional interests of the parties in the flat.

the 'trust for sale'

As shown, co-ownership may only exist behind a 'trust for sale'. The court is ready to imply such a trust where, for example, one party has contributed to the purchase price, or mortgage repayments or substantially contributed to household expenses. So, when the legal estate is conveyed to one partner, following what was a joint purchase financed partly by the other partner, a trust for sale will be implied.

This is particularly important in the context of the family home where the property is conveyed into the man's name, as often happens, but the woman claims a share in the flat. Provided that the woman can convince the court that there is an implied trust for sale, the man will hold the legal estate on trust for himself and his partner.

There are two types of implied trust: the resulting trust and the constructive trust. The basic distinction is that the resulting trust is based on the expressed or inferred intentions of the parties at the time of buying the property, whereas the constructive trust is implied to prevent what would otherwise be a 'fraud'.

the resulting trust

The resulting trust is based on the commonsense notion that a person who contributes to the purchase price expects to get something in return. Various permutations can arise: contributions can be made to the deposit and legal fees, the purchase price, the mortgage repayments, for example. The trust reflects the supposed intentions of the parties (not necessarily their actual intentions) which existed at the date of the purchase of the property.

The subsequent conduct of the parties may, however, throw light on their original intentions.

joint contributions towards the purchase price
In the situation where, for example, Ian and Lizzie both contribute to the purchase of a flat which is then conveyed into Ian's name only, there is implied a resulting trust for the benefit of both. Ian merely holds the paper title to the flat. If Ian and Lizzie have contributed unequal amounts, they are presumed to be tenants in common in proportion to their respective contributions. Where they contribute equally, the presumption is that their entitlement is as joint tenants.

EXAMPLE:
Ian and Lizzie buy a flat for £80,000 and the legal title is

vested in the name of Ian. Ian provided £20,000 in cash, Lizzie provided £60,000 in cash. Under the resulting trust, Ian has a 1/4 share and Lizzie a 3/4 share.

Their financial contribution may take the form of a direct payment of cash or the taking on of the mortgage payments.

contribution of mortgage repayments

If there is an express agreement how the mortgage repayments are to be borne by the parties, this will be evidence of their shares under the trust for sale. If there is no such agreement, the court can deduce their shares from the actual payments made by each.

contribution to the deposit and legal expenses

A money contribution to the initial 10% deposit or to conveyancing fees can give rise to a resulting trust. Unless a contrary intention can be shown, it is presumed that a co-ownership arises. As with contributions to the purchase price, the share of both parties has to be quantified and is not necessarily proportional to the exact contribution made. Much depends on what the court believes was intended.

contribution to general household expenses

David has had the property conveyed into his name and he is solely responsible for the mortgage repayments. Louise contributes to the general expenses of running the flat (such as buying furniture, food and provisions, and paying the bills). Because of this, David is able to make the mortgage repayments. Does this give rise to a resulting trust in favour of Louise? The answer is not straightforward and raises several issues.

○ General household expenditure does not, of itself, give rise to co-ownership. Only in exceptional circumstances

will such expenditure be regarded as an indirect contribution to the purchase.
○ A trust may arise where there is inferred a common intention of the parties to acquire an interest in the flat by way of such indirect payments. If this can be established, the household payments are regarded as payments towards the purchase of the flat. But a real and mutual agreement between the parties to this end has to be shown.

In the David and Louise example, Louise would have to convince the court, by referring to any correspondence and conversations, or by showing that the fact of her contribution indicates that, more likely than not, both she and David operated on the understanding that she was to acquire an interest in the flat.

The court will not imply this intention readily: Louise's argument would be strengthened if she had made some other financial contribution as well (for example, towards the deposit or legal expenses). Unless Louise can establish this extra financial input, she will find it most difficult to convince the court of the 'common intention'. This would, of course, be of great importance to Louise when the flat is to be sold.

payment of 'rent'
For money payments to bring about a resulting trust, this must be for the buying, rather than the use of, the flat. No resulting trust is implied merely from the payment of a rent, let alone ground rent. So, if Graham buys a flat in which to live with Andrew, but does not want him to acquire an ownership interest in it, it may be advisable for Graham to arrange any payments made by Andrew to be classified as 'rent'.

domestic services

Domestic labour, even over many years, does not give an interest in the property. So, if a woman stays at home to look after the children and to keep the home clean and tidy she acquires no ownership interest in the flat through this.

obstacles to the resulting trust

The trust may be negatived by a number of factors:

○ if the contribution was by way of a gift;
○ where the financial expenditure was by way of a loan;
○ if the contribution is made by the husband and the legal title is vested in the wife, an outdated notion called 'advancement' may apply. The husband will be regarded as having made a gift of the money to the wife and she will have sole ownership of the flat. The reverse does not, however, hold good: if the money is contributed by the wife and the legal title is vested in the husband, the wife will acquire an interest in the property as a co-owner. It also does not apply to an unmarried couple living together.

constructive trusts

A constructive trust is of a more far reaching nature. It involves the court in assessing the nature of the transaction and in awarding someone an interest in the property where it would be unfair not to do so. This is quite independent of the actual or presumed intentions of the parties. A mainstream example would be where the legal owner has encouraged another party to act to that party's detriment in the reasonable belief that by doing so an interest in the property would be acquired. This act can arise either before, at the time of or subsequent to the purchase of the flat.

But the claimant would have to show that he or she acted under either an express or tacit encouragement that an interest in the property would be acquired. This is where the difficulties arise in practice.

some practical solutions

If one party is to expend money towards the buying or improvement of the flat, but it is not intended that a co-ownership situation should arise, the simple way of preventing a trust being implied is by stating this in writing, signed by both parties. Any form of words would suffice provided that the intention not to give an interest in the flat is clearly spelled out, for example: 'The parties agree that the legal and beneficial title to the property is vested solely in Jim and that Jules does not acquire any interest whatsoever in the property by reason of his contributions.'

Another practical solution is for the other person not to expend money unless he gets his name on the title deeds.

the buyer's predicament

The major difficulty which a buyer faces when buying property is that he will not know if it is impliedly co-owned, because the trust for sale is not disclosed by the conveyancing documents. A buyer will often be unaware that there is anyone other than the seller with an interest in the property under a resulting or constructive trust and will therefore not be paying the money to two trustees.

Does this mean that the buyer will be bound by the rights

of occupation of the non-disclosed co-owner? The answer is, not surprisingly, somewhat complex. It primarily depends on whether the property in question is unregistered or registered.

if unregistered:
In this system of conveyancing, the buyer will be bound if he has actual, constructive or imputed notice of the beneficial interest. That means if the buyer is aware, should have been aware or his agent (for example, solicitor) knows the situation regarding the co-owner, then what he buys will be subject to the co-owner's interest.

if registered
In the case of registered land, the general rule is that a buyer will only be bound by an interest which is actually entered, and therefore protected on the Land Register. The exception to the general rule is that the rights of a co-owner in occupation of the flat will still be binding on a buyer by virtue of that occupation. (This is known as an 'overriding interest' because it overrides the consequences of non-registration.) So, provided that the other person remains in actual occupation of the flat, he or she has no need to worry because his or her interest will be binding on a subsequent buyer of the flat, even someone who does not know of anyone else living there. (The occupant can either stay on or sue the ex-partner for a share of the proceeds of the sale, in which case the buyer would remain unaffected.)

some practical solutions for the buyer

The buyer (or his solicitor) should inspect the property to see if anyone else is living there and make enquiries about this.

From a practical point of view, a buyer can avoid the problem of being saddled with the interest of an occupier by insisting on vacant possession being given before parting with the purchase money. If he suspects an undisclosed co-ownership interest, he should get the other occupier of the flat he is buying to sign a release of any interest in the property.

buying a flat for someone else

If someone who is not going to live there contributes towards the price of a flat (perhaps a parent helping out with a first purchase) there are several ways in which the interest of the contributor can be preserved.

express co-ownership

The property can be conveyed into both names, as joint tenants or tenants in common, and both would be trustees of the property. (All that has been said in the preceding pages about joint tenants and tenants in common applies even if one of the co-owners, or indeed all the co-owners, will not be living in the property.)

Where a property was bought with the help of finance from a friend or relative in this way and later the money has been repaid (or perhaps the parent has decided to make a gift of it), co-ownership will exist until the property is conveyed into the name of the occupier who then becomes the sole owner.

Another possible means of contribution is for the one who is providing the funds to do so by undertaking the repayment of the mortgage loan. This can be done by taking out a joint mortgage. In practice, the mortgagee would insist on both the names appearing on the lease or other title documents. The interest payments on £30,000 would be eligible for tax relief under MIRAS. But tax relief can be claimed only by the person(s) who occupy the mortgaged premises. It can be apportioned between them or benefit one of them only.

implied ownership

If the property is conveyed into the name of only the person who is going to live there, a resulting trust would arise. Co-ownership would therefore arise by implication (the consequences of this have been discussed).

If the title to the land is registered, it would be wise for the person who is providing part of the money to enter a restriction on the Land Register: this would warn prospective buyers that there is a co-ownership.

The unregistered system, however, offers no form of registered protection.

no co-ownership

Another possibility would be for the person who wants to help out with buying the flat to make a straight loan of the necessary amount, to be repaid either in instalments or in a lump sum at the end of a specified period. Unless it is intended otherwise, the lender does not have a charge on the property. It is not a mortgage and the lender does not acquire an interest in the flat.

If it is intended for the loan to be secured, it is advisable, by way of a safeguard for the loan, to register a charge at the Land Registry (if the property is registered) or enter a land charge if the property is not registered. For both, standard application forms have to be completed. Such transactions are probably better handled by a solicitor.

The consequence of protecting the loan by registration is that before the flat-owner can sell it to a new buyer, the charge would have to be redeemed by repaying the debt.

SERVICE CHARGES

In addition to having to pay ground rent, the lease may contain a covenant which obliges the tenant to pay an annual service charge to the landlord or management company. The landlord may be responsible for maintaining the structure and common parts but will expect to be repaid by the flat owners for the cost of doing so. The amount of the service charge will reflect the landlord's obligations under the lease. Service charges are particularly common with a block of flats.

The Landlord and Tenant Act 1985 gives tenants certain rights independent of any contractual agreement. The Landlord and Tenant Act 1987 strengthens the tenants' rights with regard to service charges and insurance arrangements.

the service charge

A service charge is an amount payable, directly or indirectly, for services (porterage and cleaning, upkeep of garden and lifts, for example), repairs, maintenance, insurance and the landlord's overheads in the management of the property. Other items cannot legitimately be dressed up as a service charge, although many leases contain a catch-all phrase.

The key issues which need to be clearly defined in the lease are

○ the obligation on the landlord to provide services;
○ to what services and expenditure the covenant extends;

○ how the expenditure is to be apportioned between the tenants;
○ the procedure for certifying the expenditure;
○ when the service charge is payable;
○ whether any provision is made for the creation of a 'sinking fund' or reserve fund.

The details will be contained in the lease along these lines:

i) "The Tenant HEREBY COVENANTS with the Landlord to contribute and pay parts [*a formula or percentage will be stated*] of the costs, expenses, outgoings and matters mentioned in the schedule hereto

ii) the contribution under paragraph (i) of this clause for each year shall be estimated by the managing agents for the time being of the Landlord (hereinafter referred to as "the managing agents") or if none the Landlord (whose decision shall be final) as soon as practicable after the beginning of the year and the Tenant shall pay the estimated contribution by two equal instalments on March 25 and September 29 in that year.

The landlord HEREBY COVENANTS with the Tenant to supply to the Tenant not less frequently than once every year a summary of the costs expenses outgoings and matters mentioned in the Schedule hereto for the previous calendar year which summary shall also incorporate statements of the amount (if any) standing to the credit of Tenant . . ."

The nuts and bolts of the charge follow in the schedule giving details of what the tenant is liable to contribute to. The schedule may mention:

○ the expenses of insurance taken out by the landlord under the lease;
○ the expenses of the landlord in carrying out his obligations under the lease regarding repairs, cleaning, painting and lighting of common parts, for example;
○ the costs incurred by the landlord for the repair and maintenance of the lift;

o the expenses of decorating the exterior and the interior common parts of the building;

o the fees and costs paid to any managing agents appointed;

o the fees and costs paid to any accountant, solicitor or other professional person in relation to audits and certification of accounts;

o all other expenses (if any) incurred by the landlord in relation to any arbitration or court action concerning the charges;

o that the landlord can employ contractors to carry out his obligations under the lease or, if he carries them out himself, claim the normal charges (including profit) for the work;

o that, unless managing agents are appointed, the landlord can claim for his own administration expenses;

o that provisional assessments and payment demands may be made;

o that a sinking fund be set up to cover the replacement of major items such as lifts and boilers in the future (so that expenditure on those items does not fall in one year);

o that the landlord may charge interest on money borrowed from the bank to carry out his repair/maintenance obligations.

the contribution formula (the apportionment)

Each flat owner has to covenant to pay as the service charge a proportion of the expenses, the total of the proportions amounting to 100% of the expenses. Sometimes certain items of expenditure are shared amongst only some of the flat owners (for example, some flats that do not have a garage while others do in a block, or ground floor occupants who do not normally use the lift, may not have to pay these upkeep expenses).

The apportionment may be calculated in a broad sense, that is, each flat owner paying the same proportion regardless of the size and position of the flat. Some schemes calculate the contribution according to rateable value or according to floor space. Whichever method is used, there will be tenants who believe that they are unfairly disadvantaged – and maybe they are.

Prospective buyers should be aware that where there is an unscrupulous or sloppy landlord or management company, the apportionments may add up to more than 100%, or they may be based on incorrect data if they are calculated on the ratios of the rateable values. In such cases, challenge the figures, and as a last resort the matter may have to go to court.

time of payment

The landlord will wish to have the service charge available to meet expenditure as it falls due. Otherwise he would have to use his own resources or borrow money (and, can only recover the interest on such credit from the tenant if the lease so provides).

The usual way of dealing with this is that the lease defines the financial year in respect of which the service charge is payable and at the end of that year the certification of the total charge is given. The tenants will be required, by their leases, to pay estimated sums on account. The most common way is by two interim payments followed by an excess service charge demand where necessary. Any adjustment is made when the total charge is calculated and the tenant will either pay the difference or be given an allowance against the next payment.

limitations

There is some limitation on the amounts that can be legitimately charged. This is laid down by law and, if necessary, enforceable in a court of law. As a general yardstick, service charges should be limited to costs reasonably incurred (in the period to which the demand relates generally retrospectively for the past year). The charges should be for services or works which are of a reasonable standard.

The tenant is free to request written details of the costs and how they have been calculated and the landlord must then respond. Such information must disclose also what bills have been paid and those that remain outstanding. The tenant is able to inspect (that is, the landlord must give him reasonable access) and copy, at the tenant's own expense, any supporting accounts.

Where a written summary of the costs is provided, it must be certified by a qualified accountant who is neither a partner nor employee of the landlord. The certification must be made even if the lease says nothing about it.

An accountant's certification may be no guarantee of arithmetical accuracy and in practice the tenants' requests for sight of the invoices is sometimes ignored.

works carried out

Where the landlord wishes to carry out works on the premises (repairs, construction and maintenance, for example), further restrictions exist. If the cost of such works is more than the greater of either £1000 or £50 × the number of flats, the landlord must consult the tenants. Otherwise, the excess cost may be irrecoverable from the tenants.

The landlord may only claim for such excess costs either with the approval of the court or when certain specified requirements are satisfied. These requirements concern estimates and consultation, unless the work is carried out in an emergency, and differ according to whether the tenants are represented by a recognised tenants' association or not.

estimates and consultation

Where the landlord wishes to carry out work above the maximum figure and no recognised tenants' association exists in relation to the building, the landlord must take the following steps:

○ obtain at least two estimates for the proposed work of which one, at least, must be from a person wholly unconnected with the landlord;
○ provide for each tenant (or display where it is likely to come to the attention of all the tenants) a notice which describes the intended works, contains a copy of the estimates and invites comments;
○ give, as a general rule, at least one calendar month's notice of the proposed works (except in emergencies);
○ have regard to any observations received. This does not mean, however, that the landlord must act on the comments provided by the tenants.

In connection with those tenants who are represented by a recognised tenants' association, the landlord must:

○ give the secretary of the association a detailed specification of the proposed works and allow a reasonable period within which the association may put to the landlord the names from whom estimates should be obtained;

○ obtain at least two estimates, one from a wholly independent person;
○ provide a copy of the estimates to the secretary of the
association;
○ give to each tenant a notice describing the works,
summarising the estimates, offering the right and opportunity to inspect and take copies of the detailed specifications of the intended works and estimates, and invite
observations;
○ have regard to any comments made by the tenants;
○ unless there are urgent safety reasons, not start the
works earlier than the date specified in the notice (usually
at least one month's advance notice).

A time limit concerning the tenant's liability is also laid
down. The tenant has to be notified of the costs during the
eighteen months following the works, otherwise he is not
liable to pay service charges for costs incurred more than
eighteen months before the demand for payment.

a trust fund

The Landlord and Tenant Act 1987 imposes a trust (in most
cases the landlord, managing agents or management
company being the trustees) on all the money paid as
service charges and on any income from investments of
those payments. The purpose of this trust fund is to defray
the costs for which the charges were raised, and, over and
above this, for the benefit of the existing tenants. The major
advantage of this is that the money is protected from the
creditors if the landlord becomes insolvent.

The lease may contain a clause setting up the trust, by

saying, for example, that any monies paid by way of service charge shall be held

> ". . . in trust for the Tenant until applied towards the Tenant's contribution towards the costs expenses outgoings and matters mentioned . . . Any interest or income of funds for the time being held by managing agents or if none the Landlord pending application as aforesaid shall be added to the funds."

Unless there are any express terms in the lease about the distribution of the trust fund, the entitlement of each tenant is proportional to his or her contribution to the service charge. When a lease is assigned, the outgoing tenant will not be entitled to a share of the fund: this share will be acquired by the incoming tenant. There is nothing to stop the outgoing tenant from asking for a payment equivalent to this amount from the incoming tenant, at the time when the contract for the assignment of the flat is negotiated.

a sinking fund

A 'sinking fund' is commonly established so as to cater for the replacement of major items such as lifts, boilers, roofs and major refurbishment of the block. So that flat owners will not be faced with too large a bill in the replacement year, sums need to be put aside to cover such longer-term contingencies and to spread the cost of major expenditure over a number of years.

The landlord or management company must invest such money, and the funds are held on trust for the current tenants. The seller of an existing lease should discover from the landlord or management company the amount of his credit in the fund and ask the buyer to pay him this sum on completion.

The lease will tell the tenant about the sinking fund and may provide that the landlord can use the fund for other service expenditure properly incurred. The lease will also prevent the flat-owners from demanding repayment. If the landlord sells the reversion, the fund will be transferred to the buyer, the new freeholder of the property.

insurance

The landlord or management company may be obliged, under a covenant, to take out buildings insurance for the whole block of flats. Where the service charge includes a payment for insurance, the tenant (or tenants' association) can require the landlord to supply written details of the insurance. These details must reveal the amount of the cover, the name of the insurer and the risks insured. The landlord may meet this request by letting the tenant have a copy of the appropriate policy.

The tenant is also given the right to inspect the original insurance policy, and the premium receipts, and to take a copy of them. If the tenant is unhappy about the policy (for example, because the premiums are excessive or the coverage inadequate), an application can be made to the court for it to order the landlord to change insurers and/or policy.

In practice, a major difficulty is to assess the value of a block of flats for the purposes of insurance coverage. The insurers themselves, and also surveyors, are sometimes unable to suggest a figure. The danger is that the block will be over-insured or under-insured. This may encourage individual flat-owners to take out further insurance (this may, moreover, be required by the mortgagee). In the event of a claim, there would be one lot of payment only.

flat owners' (or tenants') association

A tenants' association is one which is representative of the tenants and recognised as such by the landlord, the rent assessment committee, and the court. The officials of the association act as agents for the members as a whole, and the members are liable personally in respect of any obligation incurred by the association. The association will, usually, have no substantial assets.

The importance of a recognised association lies in the collective bargaining power the members have in relation to the landlord. In addition, under the Landlord and Tenant Act 1987 the association has the right to be heard on the question of major repairs before estimates are asked for. A tenants' association can act as a watch-dog to ensure that its members and the landlord abide by the covenants contained in the leases. If legal action against the landlord is appropriate, the association can initiate action on behalf of all its members. An association, recognised or not, is not a legal personality and cannot go to court. One member, however, can take representative action on behalf of all lessees even if they are non-members of the association. Tenants' associations cannot get legal aid but any or all individual tenants who are eligible under the Law Society's 'green form' scheme can get up to £50's-worth of legal advice and assistance.

The association can negotiate with the landlord over a variety of matters including the quality of services provided, their cost, the contractors to be used and the consideration of estimates, for example. Even where the landlord takes no notice of a complaint, having made it may be a preliminary to taking legal action.

The acts of the association may only bind its members (and not non-associate tenants) and, moreover, individual members can disengage themselves from the acts of the association if not in agreement. Unless such tenants notify the landlord to the contrary, however, the landlord assumes that the association has the authority to bind all its members.

recognition of tenants' association

Under the provisions of the Landlord and Tenant Act 1985, an association of residents who pay variable service charges (as long leaseholders generally do), can apply to the landlord to be 'recognised'.

Application for recognition should be made in writing and state how many flats are represented by the association. This should generally be more than 60% of the flats in the block. Send the letter by recorded delivery. If the landlord does not respond by sending a notice of recognition, the association can apply to the rent assessment committee for a certificate of recognition.

The Federation of Private Residents' Associations (11 Dartmouth Street, London SW1H 9BL, telephone 01-222 0037) has an information pack (£5) with full details, model letter, and relevant documentation.

The Federation's functions include helping to set up tenants' associations, providing legal and other advice for member associations, acting as a ginger group with regard to existing and future legislation. Amongst its publications are a quarterly newsletter, a model constitution for tenants' associations, information packs and various information sheets.

For a tenants' association to become a member of the Federation, there is a once-only registration fee (at present £40) and an annual subscription. The amount of this depends on the number of flats in the association, with a minimum subscription of £32 for a tenants' association of up to 14 flats. For an association with 15 to 87 flats, the subscription is calculated at £2.25 per member flat.

THE MANAGEMENT AND THE MANAGEMENT COMPANY

Much responsibility may fall on the landlord in connection with the maintenance and repair of the common parts and the provision of services. The expenditure will be recovered from the tenants' service charges. Unless the building consists of no more than two flats, generally there will need to be some system of management of the premises.

There are various forms that this management may take, the more common ones will now be considered.

direct management

The landlord manages the building directly or through agents, carries out the obligations of maintenance and management and is reimbursed by the revenue from ground rents and service charges. The flat owners have no say in the management of the building. Usually, the landlord employs a managing agent and the fees for such professional assistance are passed on to the tenants.

In relation to a block of flats, the landlord may be keen to be free of what is an onerous and unenviable responsibility and may look to one of the other forms of management.

management by concurrent lease

The landlord grants to managing agents a concurrent lease, interposed between the landlord and the flat-owners, so that the agents acquire the rights of the landlord for the duration of the lease, and also the obligations.

The agents should be a reputable firm (perhaps of surveyors) with sufficient assets to carry out their obligations. The flat owners should, in theory, not have to worry about this shift of responsibility. The landlord remains liable on the covenants contained in the lease to the flat owners.

The agents will receive the ground rents and the service charges (which includes their fee).

tenants' freehold-owning management company

In its basic form, the management company draws its membership exclusively from the flat owners and the landlord's reversion (the freehold) is conveyed to the company. The landlord, having disposed of the freehold, drops out of the picture (but always remains liable on his covenants).

The tenants can buy an 'off the peg' company from a firm which specialises in ready-made companies. It is up to the tenants to decide which type of company to operate: a company limited by shares, or by guarantee, or one of unlimited liability. The issue of share capital and the concept of unlimited liability are out of place in a management company. The most advisable course is to establish a company limited by guarantee.

powers and purpose of management company

The company will need to state its purpose and powers and this is done within two documents: the memorandum and the articles of the association. These normally follow a standard form and contain the following details:

the memorandum:

○ the name of the company (for example 'The Covert Management Company Limited'; it is commonly the name of the block or the street on which it is situated);
○ the object underlying the company's formation (for example, to acquire the freehold; to manage; to borrow money if necessary; to enhance the value and beneficial advantages of the building);
○ the limitation of each member's liability to a nominal sum (for example, £1);
○ the restriction of membership to flat owners.

the articles:

○ the recognition of the purposes as set out in the memorandum;
○ the cessation of membership on the sale of the flat;
○ the provision of voting rights for each member;
○ the procedure for calling annual general meetings and extraordinary general meetings and the regulation of proceedings at such meetings;
○ the election procedure for directors and the power to appoint a secretary;
○ the necessity to produce annual audited accounts and the place where those accounts are to be kept.

By virtue of a management company, the tenants can, in theory, do as they please with the building. In practice, however, to avoid disputes and to achieve unanimity, much turns on strong and effective leadership within the company.

MANAGEMENT SCHEMES

LANDLORD
Always liable on covenants.

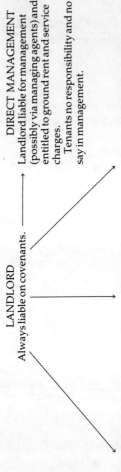

CONCURRENT LEASE

Managing Agents
Agents liable for management and on landlord's covenants. Entitled to fee, ground rents and service charges.

Tenants no responsibility and no say in management, have to look to agents if problems.

INTERPOSED LEASE

Tenants' Management Company
Company responsible for management and on landlord's covenants. Pays the landlord a ground rent, but entitled to ground rent and service charge from individual tenants.

Tenants have control of management. Individual tenants who are members of the company have limited financial liability.

Tenants have to look to company and not landlord if problems.

DIRECT MANAGEMENT
Landlord liable for management (possibly via managing agents) and entitled to ground rent and service charges.

Tenants no responsibility and no say in management.

FREEHOLD SALE

Tenants' Management Company
Company buys freehold and becomes the landlord. Directly responsible for management and entitled to ground rents and service charges. Liable on landlord's covenants. Individual members have limited financial responsibility.

Tenants exercise control over repair and maintenance of building, no longer look to landlord if problems.

who runs the shop?

The company must be run by someone and it must have directors and a secretary. Often the board of directors is elected by and from the flat owners, the secretary (usually a solicitor) being appointed by the board. An auditor will also need to be used. The fees for the professionals will be taken from the ground rents and service charges.

Normally it is desirable for the management to be placed in the hands of a professional (such as an estate agent or surveyor). The manager is appointed by the board to see to the repairs, maintenance and provision of services, and the collection of ground rents and charges. If there were no manager, that would save his fees but the burden would be likely to fall on a few conscientious flat-owners or the building might fall into neglect.

Once the freehold is vested in the company, the position of a flat owner is not really affected whether a member of the company or not. The value of any individual lease is untouched.

It is, however, usual to try to make all the flat owners become members. Pressure can be applied when existing leases are assigned and there may well be a covenant in the assignment which compels the assignee to become a member. The disadvantage of non-membership is that the tenant has no say in the running of the company and the management of the building.

Tenants who set up a freehold-owning management company should ensure that there is one share/vote per flat only and that, where some tenants do not wish to participate in the purchase of the freehold, their votes are left in abeyance. This helps to avoid dictatorships.

The individual flat owner's financial liabilities will, in practice, be the same whether a member or not, because the tenant will always have to pay the appropriate service charge.

interposed management company

It is possible for a tenants' management company to exist while the landlord still retains the freehold title and is paid the ground rent. The company takes a lease of the whole building and covenants to carry out the landlord's obligations and collect the service charge and ground rent. This is similar to being managing agents and does not affect the individual flat-owners' leases. The landlord remains liable on the covenants found in the original leases.

The flat owners, as the members of the company, have to make sure that the company can finance the day to day running of the block. A deposit may be required from each tenant to establish a float to finance initial repairs. The service charge may also be made payable in advance, with any adjustments to be made at the end of the year. It is usually desirable that a 'profit rental' be agreed with the landlord. This simply means that the company receives more in ground rent from the tenants than it pays out to the landlord. This helps to top up the company's sinking fund.

ENFORCING THE COVENANTS

As shown in earlier chapters, the covenants play a vital role in the relationship of landlord and tenant. Covenants are, however, only of value if capable of speedy and effective enforcement. Both the landlord and the tenant have a number of ways of dealing with the breach of any express or implied obligation contained in the lease. Some of these remedies benefit the landlord alone, others are open to both parties.

The general remedies for breach of covenant are an action for damages, specific performance or injunction.

action for damages

On the breach of covenant, the party in default is in breach of contract. Accordingly, it is open for the aggrieved party to sue for compensation (the words compensation and damages are interchangeable). The award is calculated, generally, on the basis of putting the aggrieved party into the position he would have been in had the covenant been complied with. This means that the court must estimate the amount of loss that the injured party has suffered. As regards a claim by the landlord, compensation cannot be more than the amount by which the value of the reversion has diminished.

Although this is rarely done, there is nothing to prevent the parties expressly stipulating in the lease a fixed amount to be paid on the breach of any one, or every, covenant. This sum must, however, constitute a genuine pre-estimate of the future loss.

specific performance

The party who seeks to compel compliance with the terms of the lease can apply to the court for the discretionary remedy of specific performance. This means asking the court to order the other party to perform the agreed contractual terms.

The remedy is, however, at the court's discretion and is not always granted and will not usually be available if compensation is an adequate redress. In practice, it is unlikely that the landlord will be granted specific performance against the tenant; the tenant does not face the same difficulty. It would be granted where it is fair and just to do so (for example, the landlord failing to maintain common parts).

an injunction

This can be sought in order to restrain the other party from breaching the contract. This remedy is also discretionary and, therefore, not available as of right.

An injunction would be appropriate to restrain the tenant from using the premises contrary to the terms of the covenants, to restrain the landlord from harassing the tenant or to prevent the tenant from assigning or subletting in breach of a covenant, for example.

The general use of an injunction is to restrain someone (via the court) from doing a certain act. There is no injunction available, however, to compel a tenant or landlord to carry out repairs. In this case, damages would prove to be an adequate remedy or, if not, specific performance of the contract could be ordered.

the landlord's remedies

The covenant to pay rent is treated differently from all the other covenants of the tenant.

the covenant to pay rent

In the case of long residential leases, it is common for only a nominal ground rent to be payable. Rent becomes due on the day stipulated for payment and is in arrears from the following day. Several sanctions can be employed against a tenant in arrears.

rent action
Rent is a debt and arrears are recoverable for up to 6 years by way of an action for breach of contract, in the county court. There is available in this court a speeded-up procedure known as a rent action.

If the tenant cannot, or refuses to, pay, the judgment needs to be enforced. There are two methods of enforcement: obtaining an attachment of earnings order and sending out the court bailiffs under a warrant of execution.

There are other actions the landlord can take for the recovery of rent arrears, such as distress and forfeiture.

distress
Distress for rent is a self-help remedy which the landlord can take generally without going to court. It allows the landlord to enter the tenant's flat (but not by force) and seize and sell goods found there. Because a long lease involves

only a small ground rent, it is unlikely that the amount of arrears is large enough to make distress worth using against long leaseholders in normal circumstances.

However, distress can be used, and sometimes is used, as a means of intimidating tenants to leave at the end of the lease.

forfeiture

This constitutes the most powerful weapon in the armoury of the landlord. It allows the landlord to 're-enter' the tenant's premises and to put an end to the lease. It is of particular relevance as regards a long lease which, unlike other types of tenancies, cannot be ended by a notice to quit. All well-drafted long leases contain a forfeiture clause, and expressly give to the landlord the right to retake possession. Forfeiture is not available unless there is such a clause.

Even where the covenant is breached, the lease does not come to an end automatically. It is the landlord who has the option to end it or to allow it to continue. Where the landlord waives his right to forfeit, he loses the right to do so for that particular breach of covenant. The non-payment of ground rent is, however, often a recurring matter and a fresh right to forfeit would arise with future arrears.

The procedure involved with forfeiture is awkward and complex. Due to its potentially far reaching effects, the remedy is the subject of major safeguards:

○ it can only be enforced against a residential tenant on the authority of the court, usually the county court;

○ the right must be expressly contained in the lease;

○ the tenant may apply to the court to stop the landlord's forfeiture (at any time up to 6 months even after forfeiture has been ordered). If forfeiture is granted, the mortgagee's security for the lease evaporates, so the mortgagee will be forewarned of the action and can apply to the court for relief. This is usually granted by the court.

Forfeiture is rare when the breach of covenant can be remedied (for example, if the arrears are paid up and costs paid). Because of this, it is uncommon for the court to grant forfeiture of a long lease for a failure to pay ground rent. Nevertheless, the threat of forfeiture can be exploited by the landlord.

breach of other covenants

The landlord has remedies concerning other breaches of contract by the tenant.

compensation for waste

The tenant may be liable to the landlord for causing any loss because of alteration to the premises by way of damage, destruction, addition, or neglect. The landlord may claim compensation for such loss through the courts.

The measure of compensation is the amount by which the landlord's reversion has been decreased in value, less some discount for the fact that payment is being made before the lease has expired.

forfeiture

The meaning and effect of this has been discussed in the context of the non-payment of rent. Different procedures need to be adopted where the breach is of another covenant.

Forfeiture for breach of a covenant other than non-payment of rent is also closely regulated by law. Before forfeiture can take place, the landlord must serve a notice on the tenant which must:

○ specify the breach complained of;
○ require the tenant to remedy it if it is capable of remedy;
○ require the tenant to pay compensation for the breach.

Most, even if not all, covenants are capable of remedy and the tenant must be given a reasonable time to comply with the notice. An example of a covenant which is irremediable is one against immoral or illegal use of the premises. Such activities are regarded as attaching a stigma to the property and, therefore, incapable of remedy.

The notice to the tenant is designed to offer a last chance to make good the default, where it is possible, rather than face the threat of loss of the lease.

In relation to forfeiture for non-compliance with a repairing covenant, further limitations are imposed. The Leashold Property (Repairs) Act 1938, which applies to leases granted originally for over 7 years and still with more than 3 years remaining, requires the permission of the court before the landlord can forfeit or sue for damages.

A tenant who receives a notice from the landlord, can counter-claim the protection of the 1938 Act. This has to be done within 28 days. The notice must inform the tenant of this right.

To take the matter further, the landlord must then apply for the permission of the court. This permission may be given only on certain prescribed grounds. The grounds as laid down by the Act include, for example, where there is an imminent likelihood of the landlord's freehold being diminished in value or where there are special circumstances to make it 'just and equitable' to allow the landlord to forfeit the lease.

The possibility remains that the court will grant relief to the tenant, that is refuse to grant forfeiture to the landlord. The court enjoys a wide discretion and may grant relief on what terms it thinks appropriate. The court may impose conditions relating to such matters as costs, expenses, compensation, for example.

As forfeiture ends the lease, this has an obvious 'knock on' effect for mortgagees (who lose the security for the loan to the tenant) and any subtenants (who lose their lease when the head lease ends). These third parties must be involved in the court action and relief will often be granted on their request.

the tenant's remedies

One remedy of self-help has emerged which assists a tenant whose landlord has failed to comply with a repairing covenant. The tenant has the right to carry out the repairs and then deduct the cost from future payments of ground rent. The principle has been extended to allowing the tenant to deduct the costs from rent arrears already in existence. (But it does not, at present, extend to withholding service charges.) This allows a tenant to withhold ground rent so as to accumulate the (albeit limited) capital sum to carry out necessary repairs which the landlord refuses to carry out.

If the landlord sues for rent arrears or attempts to levy distress, the tenant can counter-claim or resist the attempts.

withholding ground rent to pay for repairs

Although the tenant of a long leasehold usually pays only a nominal ground rent, this form of self-help may still provide a useful, even if limited, remedy for the victim of the landord's disrepair.

Several matters need to be established before the with-holding of rent can be lawful in order for the repair work to be carried out:

○ the landlord must be in breach of a repairing covenant – no room for errors here;
○ the tenant must have given notice to the landlord of the need for repair and warned him of the possible action;
○ the tenant's expenditure must be reasonable and proper. It is advisable to obtain at least two estimates regarding the work proposed and, obviously, to choose the lower (copy to the landlord).

The tenant's right to deduct from rent is not lost if there is a change of landlord.

simply withholding ground rent

The tenant has another course of action available. Instead of paying for the repairs which the landlord should have carried out, the tenant simply withholds rent and waits for the landlord to sue.

If it is unfair to allow the landlord's claim to succeed, the court will award the tenant compensation for breach of the landlord's covenant to repair.

This is known as a 'set off' or 'cross claim'. The advantage is that the tenant can recover for consequential loss arising from the disrepair and is not limited to the cost of reasonable repairs.

The advantage of these forms of self-help is that the tenant does not have to initiate court proceedings and can sit back and wait for the landlord to decide what action to take. The disadvantage is that it all takes a great deal of time during which the repairs are not done.

using a lawyer

Apart from the remedies of self-help, both parties will normally need the benefit of legal advice and, if the matter goes to court, representation. Legal services do not come cheap.

Either party may qualify for £50-worth of advice and assistance under what is known as the 'green form' scheme and apply for full legal aid. Eligibility for the two schemes is based on financial resources and both embody a means test of the applicant's earnings and capital. He may have to pay a contribution, on a sliding scale, according to the amounts of his 'disposable income' and 'disposable capital'. In such a calculation, the value of the flat is disregarded.

The danger hidden within both schemes is that the Legal Aid Board can claw back the amount spent on the case from any 'money recovered or property preserved' by the action; this is known as the 'statutory charge'.

In the full legal aid scheme, there is also a merits test which requires, essentially, that it is reasonable for the applicant to bring the case. Subject to financial eligibility, a legal aid certificate would generally be granted to defend forfeiture or possession proceedings or to bring an action against the landlord for breach of covenant.

Where there is a public sector agency offering legal advice (law centre, citizens advice bureau, housing advice centre or something similar) it may be advisable initially to make contact with such an agency. Such assistance is usually free.

FITNESS, REPAIR AND SAFETY

In a block of flats, the landlord retains possession and control of common parts and will covenant for their repair and maintenance, but the burden of repairing covenants will invariably rest heavily on the shoulders of the tenant.

Unless there is an express obligation on the landlord, no guarantee is implied by the lease that the premises will be suitable as a residence. The tenant would not have any right to complain about the fitness of the premises both when he takes the lease and when he lives in the flat. The state of the property is not guaranteed at the time the lease is granted. The prospective tenant must, as far as the flat is concerned, take it or leave it. That is why preliminary enquiries, a survey and inspection are so important before exchange of contracts.

Unless there is an agreement to the contrary, the tenant is assumed to take all risks and responsibilities connected with the future condition of the premises.

the problem of unfitness

The preservation of housing stock is obviously of social importance. The public interest suffers if repairs are not carried out because houses then decay and become dilapidated. Occupiers and adjoining neighbours will suffer also. Parliament has therefore gradually introduced laws which places some, albeit limited, obligations on the landlord to maintain and repair. It would be manifestly unjust if the responsibility was to be borne solely by the tenant.

The problem of unfit housing is acute. In London the problem is worst. But it seems that in most big cities properties are falling into disrepair faster than existing disrepair can be remedied.

the implied obligations of the landlord

Although the general rule of *caveat emptor* ('let the buyer beware') applies to flats, it does give way in certain and limited circumstances recognised by the courts and parliament. Irrespective of any express terms in the lease, certain obligations are imposed on the landlord by common law and statute.

the common law

The judges have taken somewhat hesitant steps towards establishing what constitutes a basic standard of habitation under a residential lease. This move forward has been achieved by an application of the laws of negligence and nuisance and also by implying into residential leases some contractual obligations on the landlord's part.

There is no implied undertaking by the landlord that an **unfurnished** flat is reasonably fit for habitation, unlike the USA where there is implied into every lease a warranty of habitability. Only in a lease of **furnished** premises is there an implied term that they are fit for habitation at the beginning of the lease (this will have no application to long leases because it only concerns furnished property).

As the lease is the essence of the relationship between landlord and tenant, it is by implying certain obligations of the landlord into the lease that the courts can protect the tenant's use and enjoyment of his home. Such obligations are particularly relevant to a block of flats where the landlord retains control and possession of parts of the building.

implied contractual duty of care

A duty of care is imposed on the landlord to preserve the amenities and the common parts of the building enjoyed by the tenant. The landlord is, therefore, under a duty to keep such things as lifts, rubbish chutes and stairways safe and efficient. An aggrieved tenant can apply to the court for an order compelling the landlord to carry out whatever repairs are appropriate, or if loss is suffered, seek financial compensation.

implied covenant for quiet enjoyment

There is implied into every lease a contractual obligation allowing the tenant the 'quiet enjoyment' of the premises.

This covenant is relevant not only with regard to stopping the landlord interfering, but also may help in maintaining the quality of the premises. A landlord who, for example, undertakes to maintain the roof of a building, but fails to keep it water-tight, will not only be in breach of his repairing covenant but also in breach of the implied covenant for quiet enjoyment if the tenant's flat is affected.

It would be similar if, in winter, the landlord failed to lag a water-pipe which was within the control of the landlord, and the pipe bursts and causes damage to the tenant's premises.

There would be a clear breach of the covenant (and possibly it would constitute harassment) where the landlord intentionally disconnects the tenant from mains services. The tenant may initiate civil proceedings in the county court and seek either compensation or an injunction.

liability in negligence

Irrespective of any contractual obligation, the law of negligence places on the landlord a duty to take care and expects the landlord to act as 'a reasonable man'. If there is a breach of this duty, the landlord's liability will extend to all those who are reasonably foreseeable as being affected (the tenant, the tenant's family and visitors, for example).

Although the general rule is that a landlord will not be held liable as regards defects which exist at the start of the lease, the law of negligence does have an important function in regard to damage arising from disrepair of the parts of the building retained under the control or possession of the landlord. Where, for example, the landlord retains responsibility for service ducts and common parts or the roof, but fails to clear a gutter, or to repair a down-spout or to prevent an infestation of vermin from the service ducts, the tenant could recover compensation from the landlord for damage caused by any or all of these failures.

In limited circumstances, the landlord may be held liable for damage which is caused by a third party. An example of this would be when the landlord controls a security system within the building which fails (the porter falls asleep or alarms have been ineffectively installed) and, as a result, thieves or vandals enter the flat and cause damage. In this situation, the landlord may be found liable in negligence.

liability in nuisance

The law of nuisance embraces a multitude of sins and may enable a tenant to sue the landlord where the latter unreasonably interferes with the tenant's use or enjoyment of the premises.

When a landlord leases property in a state which constitutes a nuisance, and this results in damage or injury to the tenant or his property, the landlord will be liable. Where the nuisance is caused by the act of the tenant, the landlord will usually not be liable.

This means that if the landlord remains liable under the lease for repair or maintenance of the part of the building which contains the source of the nuisance, the landlord will be accountable. The tenant's obligation to repair that part of the building, will, however, often be conclusive to show that the landlord is not liable.

The landlord will be responsible for a nuisance (for example noise, fumes, smells, damp, infestation) arising from parts of the building retained by him.

As with negligence, the tenant would need to establish fault on the part of the landlord and show loss (interference with comfort and/or physical damage or injury). Unlike negligence, only the tenant, not his visitors, for example, can bring a legal action.

The landlord will not generally be responsible for a nuisance caused by another tenant.

some helpful statutes

A series of piecemeal statutory provisions are available to assist a tenant to compel a landlord to improve the condition of the building. This legislation is so fragmented that it has been criticised as a dog's dinner which badly needs to be overhauled and consolidated. Many of the provisions do not apply to long leases, but those that have relevance include:

liability under the Defective Premises Act 1972

The Act places on the landlord, in certain circumstances, an obligation to take reasonable care to prevent damage to property which might be caused by defects in the premises leased. This duty applies only when the landlord has agreed a repairing covenant or where he has a right to enter the premises and carry out repairs if the tenant fails in his duty to do so.

The duty arises only if the landlord actually knew, or a reasonable landlord ought to have known (by inspection, for example), of the disrepair.

The defect may be one which exists at the start of the lease or may emerge subsequently. The landlord must, however, have failed to take reasonable care in respect of repair and maintenance before liability can arise.

The liability of the landlord cannot be excluded by any 'exclusion' notice or term in the contract.

liability under the Health & Safety at Work Act 1974

Although not necessarily what the parliamentary draftsmen intended, aspects of this legislation apply to residential leases. A duty is imposed on the person who has control of the premises 'in connection with the carrying on by him of a trade, business or other undertaking'. This includes an individual landlord (or, as is often the case, a management company) of a block of flats. The duty is to take reasonable care to ensure that all means of access and exit on the premises, together with "plant or substance . . . provided for use" on those premises, are safe and without risk to health.

So what does all this mean? The courts have interpreted this legislation imaginatively and have applied the duty to a landlord in order to find liability for unsafe lifts and the dangerous state of common parts.

Where the landlord ignores the repair and maintenance of such amenities as lifts and stairways and electrical installations in the common areas, for example, the tenant may request the local authority to serve an 'improvement notice' on the landlord which will compel the landlord to discharge the obligations. If the notice is issued and the landlord ignores it, he commits a criminal offence.

the Control of Pollution Act 1974

This Act regulates noise pollution and gives the local authority the power, on the complaint of the tenant to the environmental health officer of the local authority, to issue an 'abatement notice' in respect of any 'noise amounting to a nuisance'. The notice will be served on the person responsible for the nuisance and will require that the nuisance is terminated. Failure to comply with the notice is a criminal offence.

In the context of the landlord and tenant relationship, it was decided that the landlord of a building in which the lifts made an excessive noise and disturbed the tenants fell within the scope of the Act.

The Act may be used also against another flat-owner to stop noise and disturbance – but not directly. It would be a case of informing the environmental health officer and hoping that the complaint was heeded.

the Public Health Act 1936

This offers a further avenue of redress for the tenant and is another situation in which the local authority may intervene in cases of alleged housing disrepair. Any premises that are in such a condition as to be prejudicial to health (for example, defective wiring, extensive damp and mould) or to constitute a nuisance (an unreasonable interference with the enjoyment and use of the tenant's flat) fall within the definition of a statutory nuisance contained in the Act.

In this instance, it is not the defect which is the nuisance, but rather its consequences which are important. Take, for example, the case of a defective roof. The disrepair itself is not the statutory nuisance, but if the roof leaks, and the water damages the tenant's flat, this would constitute the nuisance. The Act, therefore, has importance where the landlord retains control or possession of some part of the building and the damage emanates from that part.

The tenant has two possible ways of getting redress. First, he may go direct to the magistrates' court for a 'nuisance order'. This would be appropriate where the local authority is slow to act. The tenant can 'lay an information' before the court and commence proceedings privately. Legal aid is not available, but the tenant's reasonable expenses must be paid by the other side (if he is successful). The magistrates can also make a compensation order of up to £1000 in favour of the tenant.

Second, the tenant may complain to the Environmental Health Department of the local authority and is entitled to have the complaint investigated. Where the complaint is substantiated, the local authority will serve notice on the landlord (this is not necessary when the individual goes privately and directly to the magistrates' court). This notice will specify the nuisance and may require the landlord to carry out stipulated repairs. A failure to comply will result in the landlord being made the subject of a magistrates' nuisance order and, eventually, criminal prosecution.

The local authority is given the option, in an urgent case, to by-pass the magistrates' court and to carry out the necessary repairs itself and, subsequently, bill the landlord.

which remedy?

The advantage of those remedies which involve the local authority is that the tenant does not have to incur the expense of hiring a solicitor and may not have the inconvenience of attending court. Legal aid may be available for a tenant. Unless compensation is sought, however, it may be more effective and convenient to let the local authority do the leg work. Other action which can be taken by the local authority is considered in the next chapter.

trouble with neighbours?

The law protects an occupier against nuisance and annoyance caused by the actions of others. So, if a neighbour makes too much noise or commits other forms of annoyance, the tenant may be able to go to court and sue for compensation or ask for an order (an injunction) restraining that neighbour. The order may restrict the neighbour's actions (for example, piano playing) to certain hours of the day. A practical difficulty is that the court may not be interested in anything less than loud amplified music and may require a detailed account of the disturbance over a number of weeks.

If the neighbour fails to comply with the order, the court can jail him for contempt of court.

These issues are governed by the law of nuisance, through which the occupier is protected against interference with the personal enjoyment of the flat. The court has to decide whether the neighbour's actions were reasonable or not and, to do so, must adopt a broad 'give and take' approach. In relation to noise, the court may take into acount expert evidence as to decibel readings.

A barking dog can cause further problems. Annoyed neighbours may face the distressing task of obtaining a dog destruction order from the magistrates's court.

A tenant who annoys his neighbours faces further risks. The landlord could attempt to terminate the lease prematurely by way of forfeiture for breach of covenant or, if the tenant is hanging on in occupation after the lease has expired, the nuisance may give the landlord grounds for an eviction order.

safety in the home

An Englishman's home may be his castle, but it is also a potentially hazardous place. Countless domestic accidents occur each year and most accidents involving children arise in the protective confines of their homes. As a general principle, it is the tenant, and not the landlord, who is liable for injury caused on the premises leased. There are, however, circumstances at law where the landlord, or someone else, will be liable.

liability of the landlord

Into every lease there is implied a contractual duty of care which requires the landlord to ensure a reasonable standard of safety in those areas over which control or possession is retained. This can offer an avenue of redress for the tenant who suffers physical injury due to the unsafe condition of a landlord's part of a building. A tenant who is injured, for example, by a fall on a dilapidated staircase or by tripping over a loose carpet in an unlit entrance hall might recover damages. The landlord's liability to the tenant extends not only to concealed defects, but also to those which are obvious. A landlord could, therefore, be liable for the failure to clean a snow covered step or an icy path. But only a party to the contract (the tenant alone, not a visitor) can claim.

Under negligence, however, ayone who is affected can claim.

negligence

If the landlord retains control over any part of the building, such as lifts, entrance hall, forecourt or other common parts, he will be regarded as an 'occupier' of those areas. Under the Occupiers Liability Act 1957, an occupier owes to all visitors a 'common duty of care', that is a duty to make anyone who is lawfully there safe in using the premises. The degree of safety which the landlord has to ensure is higher for children than adults: the landlord must be prepared for children to be less careful than adults.

The landlord may attempt to avoid responsibility by displaying an exclusion notice (that is, a statement that the landlord accepts no responsibility for loss or injury incurred on the premises howsoever caused). Such notices are ineffective as regards death or personal injury. As regards damage to property (which is what is meant by 'loss' in this context), they are effective only provided that they can be shown to be reasonable.

If the landlord has leased the whole of the building, and retains no part of it, he has ceased to be an occupier and the burden falls on each tenant or the management company (if appropriate).

A non-occupying landlord will, however, remain liable under the next type of liability to be discussed.

liability under the Defective Premises Act 1972

The Act imposes on the landlord a duty to take reasonable care to prevent any personal injury which might be caused by the landlord's default in the discharge of the obligations of repair and maintenance. The landlord's liability extends to anyone who might reasonably be expected to be affected (such as the tenant's family and visitors as well as to the tenant). For the duty to arise, however, the landlord must either be under an obligation to repair or maintain the premises (this could be by virtue of a repairing covenant, or some statutory provision) or else be entitled to enter the premises to carry out such work if the tenant fails to do so.

Where a tenant is injured by tripping over an uneven paving stone or when a communal garden wall collapses, for example, the landlord will be liable even if the danger had been caused by faulty repair work of a previous tenant. For liability to arise, the injury must be due to disrepair and the landlord must know, or ought to have known, of the danger.

liability of the tenant

It is generally the tenant (as occupier) on whom liability is likely to rest if anyone is injured in the flat.

As occupier, the tenant will be subject to the Occupiers Liability Act and also liable in respect of any nuisance on the premises leased.

The tenant is also under a duty to take reasonable care to ensure that the premises leased do not deteriorate so as to become dangerous to adjoining property (for example, an adjacent flat) or dangerous to anyone who is lawfully there (for example, to maintain plumbing installations, remedy damp and keep the roof and guttering in repair).

DISREPAIR: FURTHER LOCAL AUTHORITY ACTION

The Housing Act 1985 sets out to ensure that buildings (including flats) used for residential purposes meet certain basic standards. The general yardstick is that the premises must be fit for human habitation. Houses and flats which are unfit for habitation should be either repaired or withdrawn from domestic use.

The local authority is obliged to inspect its area from time to time in order to decide whether any action under the Act is necessary. The Secretary of State can compel a local authority to make its inspections, if appropriate. The authority faced with evidence of unfitness has a number of courses of action available. The authority is also given broad powers to enter premises to carry out its inspection or, where relevant, to carry out repairs.

The Act covers several other areas which are of related concern:

○ the prevention of housing in serious disrepair from deteriorating further;
○ action to remedy conditions which are a material interference with the comfort of a tenant;
○ slum clearance projects;
○ the declaration of improvement areas;
○ the award of improvement grants.

Some of these provisions may involve a tenant being temporarily or permanently displaced from the flat and, accordingly, a scheme for rehousing and compensation is contained in the Act.

unfitness for human habitation

Premises are unfit for human habitation if they are defective in one or more of the following: repair, stability, damp, internal arrangement, natural lighting, ventilation, water supply, drainage and sanitary provisions, cooking facilities and the disposal of water. There is no legal requirement for a dwelling to have a bathroom, inside lavatory, hot water system or modern wiring system. The required standards of fitness are not particularly high. But major defect in one of these areas, or several small defects, may amount to the flat being regarded as unfit for occupation. The disrepair or defect must either prevent the flat from functioning as a residence or constitute a danger or serious inconvenience to the tenants.

Once a flat is deemed unfit, the responsibility for the next move lies with the local authority. Two ways of proceeding are open to the authority: a 'repair' notice and a 'time and place' notice.

the repair notice

Unless the flat cannot be rendered fit for habitation at a reasonable cost, the authority must serve a repair notice. (The presumption, however, is that the flat can be put in a habitable condition at a reasonable price.)

The notice will be served on the tenant of a long lease as the person having control of the flat. If the whole building is unfit, the notice should be served on all long leaseholders.

In calculating whether the work can be undertaken at a reasonable cost, the local authority (and, if there is dispute, the county court), must have regard to the value of the flat in its present state, the expenditure required and the value of the premises when repaired. If the flat is beyond repair and the tenant is eventually evicted following a court order for possession, the courts are aware that this would be an unjustified windfall for the landlord. Tenants are therefore protected by the court weighing up the ultimate value of the building against the normally very high cost of repairs.

The local authority's notice must specify the works which are necessary to render the premises fit. The authority may order repair to the shell of the building, the treatment of rotten timbers and the construction of a new bathroom, for example. Sufficient details have to be provided so that a builder can offer an estimate of cost. A 'reasonable period' is given in which the works are to be carried out.

Depending on the repair covenants in the lease, it may be that the tenant will have to foot the bill. The attraction, however, is that the tenant will have the absolute right to a local authority improvement grant. This would help some-one who was brave enough, for example, to take on the lease of a dilapidated flat.

The notice allows the flat-owner to lodge an appeal. If there is no appeal and the notice is not complied with, the authority may itself enter and carry out the works. It can recover the costs from the tenant or the landlord depending on their respective repair and maintenance obligations.

the 'time and place' notice

If the flat cannot be rendered fit at a reasonable cost, the authority must take more stringent measures. A notice must be served on all persons with an interest in the property (landlord, tenants and mortgagees, for example) which states the time and the place where the future of the premises is to be discussed. The time must be not less than 21 days from the service of the notice. The purpose of this meeting is to induce the tenant or landlord voluntarily to undertake the necessary repairs.

If no such undertaking emerges, the authority must seek assurance that the premises will not be used as a residence; or make a demolition or closure order (demolition is inappropriate where one flat is in issue); or initiate compulsory purchase proceedings of the whole building.

If the undertaking or closure order involves the tenant having to move out, the tenant may have rights to be rehoused and for compensation from the local authority.

substantial disrepair

A tenant can complain to the local authority that the flat is in a state of disrepair for which the landlord is responsible and that either substantial repairs are necessary to bring it up to a reasonable standard or its condition interferes materially with the personal comfort of the tenant. Substantial repairs are large items of repair or a collection of smaller items.

If the authority is satisfied on either point, it has the discretion to serve a repair notice on the landlord. This is a power, not a duty to act. The premises must be capable of being repaired at a reasonable cost, that means the building/flat must be worth the cost of the repairs.

In relation to an allegation of interference with personal comfort, a notice may only be issued on the request of a tenant with a lease with less than 21 years to run from the time of the notice.

clearance areas

Slum clearance is a last resort method of dealing with large sections of unfit housing. It is clearly a potential threat to tenants in a run-down area. The scheme is that the local authority compulsorily purchases the buildings and demolishes them. Certain pre-conditions must be satisfied, however, before the declaration of a clearance area can be made:

○ houses in the area must be unfit for human habitation; or be dangerous or injurious to the health of the occupiers because of the bad arrangement of the premises; and
○ other buildings in the area are also so dangerous or injurious; and
○ the satisfactory method of dealing with the problem is to demolish all the buildings within the area (it is policy to try and exclude 'fit' buildings from the clearance area); and
○ the local authority has the finances to carry out such a programme; and
○ the authority can house any displaced tenants.

Before the properties are subject to compulsory purchase, there will usually be a public enquiry into the proposals. Tenants and owner-occupiers will be entitled to re-housing and compensation.

compulsory improvement

There are two further situations in which a local authority may require the improvement of a dwelling, even if it is not in a state of disrepair or unfitness. These are where the premises are in a local authority 'action area' or a 'general improvement area' and the property is lacking in one of the standard amenities. Such amenities include a fixed bath or shower, a wash basin and a sink (both supplied with hot and cold water) and a toilet. The flat must have been built or converted after 3 October 1961 and the dwelling must be capable of being brought up to standard at a reasonable cost. In such cases, grant aid is more readily available for the tenant to finance the improvements. If the grant is refused, written reasons must be provided to the applicant.

It must be remembered that most grants are at the discretion of the local authority.

grant aid

It is difficult to state with precision the type, extent and amount of financial assistance which is available from the local authority. The schemes are being constantly revised and the provisions which regulate them are extremely complex, so it is essential to check the current regulations at the time of the application. It is also advisable that no work be carried out prior to the application being considered. Due to the shifting nature of this area of the law and procedure, only the broadest outline of the grant system can be given.

To claim a grant, the applicant must own the freehold or, generally, a fixed term lease with at least 5 years remaining unexpired.

intermediate grants

This type of grant is available to secure the installation of standard amenities (toilet, sink, fixed bath or shower, for example) and, in connection with a flat, provide for the exclusive use of such amenities. It is necessary for the amenities to have been lacking for a period of 12 months before the application.

The grant is mandatory, that means that the local authority has no choice but to provide it if the conditions are fulfilled.

improvement grants

These are available at the discretion of the authority either to convert a house into flats or for improvement works over and above those covered by the intermediate grant. (Improvement, for this purpose, includes alterations and extensions). The grant is also for repair or replacement necessary to put the property in reasonable repair, so as to offer satisfactory housing for 30 years and meet certain standards of construction and physical condition. Generally no more than 50% of the grant can be used for repair, but if substantial and structural repair is necessary, up to 70% may be so used.

repairs grant

In relation to pre-1919 properties, there is a discretionary grant to finance substantial and structural repairs. But if the local authority serves a notice requiring compulsory improvement in relation to any premises, the grant is mandatory. The dwelling must be put into reasonable repair by the proposed works. This grant does not cover improvements.

special grant

This grant is available only where the building is in multiple occupation (a block of flats, for example) and is a dis cretionary award to the flat owner designed to make possible the installation of basic amenities, fire escapes and related repairs.

In some cases, however, the grant is mandatory: where the local authority requires the compulsory execution of the works or the installation of a fire escape.

Again, the authority must be satisfied that, on the completion of the works, the building will be in reasonable repair.

common parts grant

This is available to finance the improvement or repair of common parts in a building containing flats. It is discretionary. The claimant can be the landlord or the tenant and the grant is dependent on at least 3/4 of the flats in the building being occupied.

how much?

The amount of the grants depends on a combination of which grant is applied for, the works required, the eligible expenditure and the appropriate percentage to which the grant applies.

Even where an application is successful, much financial responsibility remains with the applicant. Complex formulae are used in order to calculate the percentage of the bill which the local authority will foot. The calculations differ according to the type of the property and in which part of the country it is situated. Grants are often paid by instalments.

NEW STEPS IN THE RIGHT DIRECTION

During a tenant's ownership of the flat, the covenants and their enforcement are only as effective as their wording in the lease is accurate and certain. There may be disagreement between the tenants and the landlord/management company as to the need for repair; uncertainty and delay can arise due to unclear wording of the repair covenants. There may be complications concerning who is to pay for the work and to what extent.

The Landlord and Tenant Act 1987 offers some help. The Act gives the tenant limited rights:

○ to have a manager appointed to take control of the building;
○ to make a compulsory purchase of the landlord's freehold estate;
○ to have the court vary the terms of a 'defective' or 'problem' lease.

The Act takes some important steps forward and goes some way to assisting tenants who experience problems with their landlord.

appointment of a manager

The Act introduces a new and relatively simple procedure whereby the tenant can apply to the county court for an order appointing a manager to take over control of the premises from the landlord and/or to act as receiver of ground rents and service charges. The basic idea is that, when a landlord is in default, a manager can take over responsibility for the building and rectify the default.

preliminary matters

Before the application for an order can be made, the tenant(s) must, generally, serve a notice on the landlord specifying in detail the nature of the complaint and notifying the intention to apply for a manager order.

Where the breach by the landlord is capable of remedy (for example, getting necessary work done), a reasonable time must be offered in which the situation can be rectified and the notice must make it clear that no further action will be taken if the breach is remedied. The court does, however, have the discretion to dispense with the notice where its service is not reasonably practicable (for example, where the landlord cannot be traced).

Once any period specified in the tenant's notice has expired, the court can be asked to make a management order.

the order

An order is made only where the court is satisfied that the landlord is in breach of a repair or maintenance covenant in the lease, the breach is likely to continue and it is just and convenient to make the order, or that there exist other circumstances which make the order just and convenient.

It is anticipated that the order will be used only as a last resort and there is as yet little guidance offered to the court concerning how to exercise this new power.

The order may be permanent, of limited duration, or suspended in effect. The order, if granted, will appoint the manager, provide for the manager's remuneration (the tenants and landlord may be jointly liable for this payment) and state the general functions which are to be carried out. The manager's functions will include repair, maintenance and insurance.

The order may be revoked or varied subsequently at the request of either landlord or flat-owner(s).

the problem

The manager order offers no assistance where the landlord has insufficient funds to finance the repairs, etc. The order may, however, have value because it could be followed by an acquisition order allowing the tenants to make a compulsory purchase.

acquisition order

The Act allows certain tenants compulsorily to purchase their landlord's freehold. This order is likely to be used only in exceptional cases of neglect and abuse and when the building is in a severe state of disrepair. This is perhaps not an attractive bargain to enter.

The court may make an acquisition order only if it is satisfied that this is appropriate and either

○ the landlord is in breach of the obligations concerning repair, maintenance, insurance or management of the premises, and that breach is likely to continue, and the appointment of a manager would not be an adequate remedy; or
○ for the three years before the application a manager order was in force.

To apply to the court, the tenants must be long lease-holders of flats and must constitute a majority of the flat owners in the building. Notice needs, generally, to be served on the landlord giving notification of the proposed application. The court has discretion, however, to make a compulsory purchase order even if no notice was given or the notice given is in some way defective.

who buys and at what price?

The tenants nominate a person(s) or company to whom the property is to be conveyed and the terms of the purchase should be agreed between the landlord and tenants. If the parties cannot agree the terms, the rent assessment committee works out the terms for them. The basis for this must be what is fair and reasonable. If they cannot agree about the price, it will be set by the court according to the open market value of the premises (reduced to take account of no vacant possession being offered because of the occupation of the flats).

The order ends any interest the landlord held in the premises. If the landlord cannot be found, the order can still be made.

variation of leases

Before the Act came into effect, variation of a lease proved costly because it had to be done via the High Court, unless the landlord consented. Also, there was no method which readily catered for multiple variation of leases.

The Act introduces fundamental change because it allows the county court to amend a defective lease where there is an absence of consent. Variation may be made on the application of any party to a long lease.

The grounds on which the application may be based are that the defective lease fails to make satisfactory provision on one or more of the following matters:

○ the repair or maintenance of the flat or the building;
○ the insurance of the premises;
○ the repair or maintenance of any installations and/or the provision of any services reasonably necessary to ensure that the occupiers have a reasonable standard of accommodation;
○ the recovery of expenditure incurred for the benefit of the other party (for example, insurance, service charges and legal expenses);
○ the computation of the service charge payable under the lease.

Tenants should be aware that any variation which increases the obligation of the landlord is likely to result in higher service charge for the tenants.

multiple variation

Where the tenants share the same landlord, even if they are in different buildings, the court may vary all the leases even where the leases are not identical.

Before the court can make a single order varying two or more leases (in the same building or otherwise), the application must be supported by at least 75% of the parties concerned and not opposed by more than 10%. If there are fewer than nine leases involved, all or all but one of the parties must consent.

the power to vary

The court can vary the lease as it sees fit (but cannot terminate the landlord's choice of insurer or right to nominate one). There are, however, no guidelines to help the court's decision to vary. The general rule is that a variation order will be made unless it will substantially prejudice

○ the landlord or tenant; or
○ any other person and compensation is an inadequate recompense; or
○ it would otherwise be unreasonable to grant the order.

Any variation order binds the parties to the lease(s) and other interested parties (for example, previous assignors of the lease(s)). Any other interested party may join in the proceedings and compensation can be ordered for any person who suffers loss by reason of the variation. A memorandum of any variation made will, usually, be endorsed on the lease(s).

the right to information

The Act also introduces some reforms intended to promote better communication between the landlord and the tenant. Any written demands for the payment of rent or service charges now have to contain the name and address of the landlord. If that address is not in England or Wales, the demands must also include an address in England and Wales for the service of notice and proceedings. If the demand does not contain this information, the service charge element of the demand can be ignored until such time as the information is provided.

The landlord is obliged also to provide to the tenant his (the landlord's) name and address (and, if a company, the name and address of every director and of the secretary of the company) within 21 days of a written request.

If the landlord sells the freehold, the new landlord is obliged to give the tenant written notice of the transaction and particulars (name and address) within two months. The Act adds the responsibility that the old landlord must also ensure that the details of the new landlord are provided to the tenant. Until such notification is made, the old landlord will continue to be liable alongside the new one under the lease.

When the Land Registration Act 1988 comes into force, anybody will be able to make a search at a District Land Registry to discover the name and address of the freeholder of a property.

ENDING THE LEASE

While the lease is in existence the tenant is, to all intents and purposes, the owner of the flat. The landlord has no right to enter the premises unless it is to follow up a right given to him in the lease (for example a right to view the state of repair) and cannot sell to anyone else the right to occupy the premises. Meanwhile, the tenant remains liable to observe the terms of the lease throughout its duration (to pay ground rent and to observe the other covenants). It is important to know how and when a lease is terminated.

Leases can come to an end in a variety of ways. In relation to a lease for a fixed term, the lease will usually continue until the term of years granted expires. It is, however, possible for a long lease to be terminated prematurely by forfeiture on the default of the tenant or by one party buying the other out (merger and surrender).

expiry of time

A fixed term lease will end automatically when the last day of its stated duration expires. The lease, when drafted, sets out the duration of the term of years agreed, and its starting date. The exact date of expiry, if not expressly stated, can easily be calculated. A lease granted for 110 years from 4 January 1988 will not automatically expire until 5 January 2098.

The contractual relationship terminates at the end of the period of the lease without either party having to do anything.

Although the landlord may wish the tenant to vacate the flat after midnight on January 4/5, the tenant will, due to the provisions of the Landlord and Tenant Act 1954, generally be able to remain in lawful occupation. The security of tenure of a tenant holding on after the contractual expiry of the lease will be considered in the next chapter.

forfeiture

As mentioned in a previous chapter dealing with enforcements of covenants, the landlord has the opportunity of ending the lease prematurely when the tenant is in breach of a covenant contained in the lease. Most leases contain a forfeiture clause which allows the landlord to put an end to the lease.

Forfeiture is hedged with technicalities and complexities and, moreover, is often not granted by the court. The natural tendency of the court is, as far as possible, to assist the tenant and not allow forfeiture. Although it is a means of early termination, forfeiture is an unpopular and often unsuccessful avenue for the landlord to pursue.

merger and surrender

A merger occurs when the tenant buys out the landlord's freehold (for example under an option to purchase or following a right of first refusal). The general rule is that when the landlord's and tenant's ownerships merge, the lease comes to an end and the landlord's reversion is said to 'drop down' and 'drown' the tenant's lease. Merger however does not affect underleases.

A clause will be inserted into the conveyance of the freehold to read something like:

> "The purchaser as the owner of the fee simple estate and of the leasehold estate in the Property declares that from the date of this deed the Lease shall no longer continue in force but shall be merged in the fee simple".

Merger can only be at the tenant's instigation; the landlord can never force the tenant to buy the freehold.

surrender

Surrender is the mirror image of merger. It occurs where the tenant voluntarily lets the landlord get back the lease. It may be difficult to imagine a situation where this would appeal to a tenant who has laid out a substantial capital sum in order to buy the flat. Nevertheless, there are several reasons why this may benefit the tenant. First, the landlord may buy out the tenant's interest for a hefty sum of money. Second, the remainder of a fixed term lease may be surrendered on the basis that the landlord grants a longer lease in return. Third, at the fag-end of a once long lease, the tenant may wish to give up possession voluntarily rather than defend forfeiture proceedings for breach of a repairing covenant.

For surrender, the landlord must be prepared to accept the lease back. Surrender can only occur with the joint agreement of the landlord and tenant and cannot result from the unilateral act of one party. The surrender should normally be contained in a deed drawn up by a solicitor signed by the tenant. No special wording is required as long as the intention to give up the lease is clear.

As with the operation of merger, a surrender does not destroy the rights of subtenants.

WHEN TIME HAS RUN OUT

A fixed term lease must, at some stage, expire. When this happens, the contractual relationship between landlord and tenant ends. While the lease has many years to run, this is of little concern to the tenant: the lease will be readily marketable and the prospect of potential homelessness is a distant matter. The problem emerges at the fag end of a long lease where the occupier must face the imminent possibility of losing the flat and an expensive claim for any dilapidation to put the property back into repair.

The problems which arise when a lease has approached the fag end of its term should not be underestimated. Mortgage finance from an institutional lender will, generally, not be available to a potential buyer when a lease has only 45 years or less to run. As a consequence, the lease can generally only be sold to a cash purchaser.

Also, credit is unlikely to be advanced to the tenant to carry out any major repairs. Tenants stranded in such flats will rarely have the inclination, nor may they have the money available, to effect necessary repairs and maintenance. The liability of the tenant to undertake such works will, however, continue under the covenants of the lease.

At common law, the tenant is obliged to give up possession of the flat to the landlord and there may be a covenant in the lease to this effect. The tenant, however, may benefit from some statutory protection which allows him to continue lawfully in possession even after the long lease has ended.

the Landlord and Tenant Act 1954

A lease will fall within the protection afforded by this legislation if it is a long lease (that is, granted originally for a term of over 21 years) at a low rent. A low rent is one which is less than 2/3rds of the rateable value of the premises. Most long leases fall within this classification. A further condition is that the lease would have fallen within the Rent Act 1977 had the rent not been low. This means that:

○ the flat was 'let as a separate dwelling'. Although there is much mystery as to the meaning of these 5 words, long residential leases will nearly always fall within the requirement;

○ the flat must fall within the appropriate limits of rateable value. This entails that the rateable value must not exceed £1500 in Greater London and £750 elsewhere. The majority of leases for flats will fall within these limits;

○ the tenant must occupy the premises wholly, or in part, as a residence. This is self-explanatory;

○ the lease must not otherwise be exempted from Rent Act protection. Such exemptions will usually have no relevance to long leases, with one important exception. A non-purpose built block of flats will be outside the scope of both the Rent Act and the Landlord and Tenant Act if part of the premises is the residence of the landlord.

It is apparent, therefore, that long leases will generally fall within the scope of the Landlord & Tenant Act 1954.

the protection

The importance of the 1954 Act is that it allows the court to grant a possession order, necessary for the lawful eviction of a tenant, only on limited grounds, namely where:

○ the tenant has failed to pay rent or observe the terms of the lease concerning insurance or the payment of rates; or

○ the tenant has caused a nuisance or an annoyance, or has been convicted of using the premises for an illegal or immoral purpose, or allowed them to be so used; or

○ the landlord, the landlord's adult children, parents or parents-in-law reasonably require the premises for their own occupation; or

○ there is suitable alternative accommodation available for the tenant; or

○ the landlord proposes, for the purpose of re-development after the expiry of the lease, to demolish or reconstruct the whole or a substantial part of the premises.

If the landlord fails to establish any of the prescribed grounds for possession, the tenant is entitled to remain in possession (that means: go on living there). By complicated legal logic, the end product is that the tenant will have security of tenure and pay a periodic rent determined by the rent officer. A new periodic lease will, therefore, arise under statute.

The tenant at the end of a long tenancy is, therefore, automatically allowed to remain in possession as a statutory tenant unless and until the landlord obtains a possession order.

when the landlord wants the flat back

To prevent the protection under the 1954 Act arising at the end of the long lease, the landlord must serve a notice of termination at least 6 months, but less than 12 months, in advance. This notice must state the ground on which the landlord claims possession. If the tenant remains in possession and/or serves a counter-notice electing to remain in possession, the landlord has to apply to the court for a possession order. If the landlord is successful, the tenancy will be at an end and the tenant evicted. Where the landlord fails to convince the court, the lease continues on new terms either agreed by the parties or fixed by the court. The tenant can remain in the flat indefinitely on a periodic tenancy.

This, of course, is not as good as having a fixed term lease, but it is better than being put out on the street. A shrewd tenant, at the end of the long lease, may seek to negotiate a substantial capital sum by way of an inducement to leave the flat. This may be the only way the landlord can get vacant possession of the property. Alternatively, the tenant may be able to negotiate a new lease from this vantage point.

. . . and when he does not

Where the landlord does not wish to recover possession, he may agree that the tenant should have a new tenancy. For this there is no need, generally, to go to court.

The notice given to the tenant will contain proposals for the terms of the new periodic tenancy.

The parties will agree the terms of the new tenancy between them, but where they cannot agree, application will need to be made to the court. The court will then work out the contractual provisions of the new tenancy and attempt to strike a reasonable balance between the interests of the landlord and of the tenant.

when the tenant wants to go

It may be that the tenant does not wish to stay in the flat beyond the end of the long lease. In this case, the Act requires that 1 month's notice be given to the landlord. This notice can be timed so as to expire on the exact date on which the long lease ends.

the Protection from Eviction Act 1977

This Act protects tenants of residential premises by making the unlawful eviction or harassment of the occupier a criminal offence.

To prove harassment, the tenant must satisfy the court (usually the magistrates' court) that the landlord held a positive intention to cause the tenant – whether during, or at the end of, the lease – to give up occupation or to restrict the tenant's rights. There must be some calculated act on the part of the landlord and not simply inactivity. Harassment can take many and varied forms: threats, nuisance, intimidation, deliberate failure to do necessary repairs, changing the locks.

The Act entails that a tenant holding on to possession at the end of a long .ease under the 1954 Act can be evicted lawfully only on the authorisation of the court. Any attempts to circumvent this route will make the landlord liable to criminal and civil proceedings. It is not, however, unlawful for the landlord to accept the tenant's voluntary surrender of the premises before or at the expiry of a long lease, or to buy the tenant's co-operation with a financial inducement.

When the Housing Bill 1988 is enacted, the tenant's position with regard to harassment and eviction will be strengthened.

the Leasehold Reform Act 1967

This is a complicated piece of legislation which allows certain leaseholders either compulsorily to purchase the freehold or, less popularly, acquire a 50 year extension to the original lease.

If the option to buy the freehold is taken up, the procedure to establish a 'fair' purchase price can be costly and complex where it involves the tenant in proceedings with a Lands Tribunal hearing. Where the tenant takes up the 50-year extension of the lease, he may be faced with an upward revision of his ground rent, up to many times the amount.

The Act operates to benefit the tenant of a house under a long lease at a low rent. As a flat is not a house, the Act does not assist tenants of a residential flat. There is a movement towards change and it is likely that, in future years, legislation will be introduced to bring the treatment of flats into line with that of houses.

OPTIONS AND PRE-EMPTIONS

The lease may contain a clause which allows the tenant an option to renew a long lease at the end of its term or to buy the landlord's freehold. Or the tenant may be given, in the lease, the right of first refusal (pre-emption) if the freehold is subsequently put on the market.

If not in the lease, an option to renew or a right of pre-emption can be negotiated between tenant and landlord and, if agreed, be put as a clause in a written contract.

In some situations, a statutory right of pre-emption arises under the Landlord and Tenant Act 1987.

options to renew

A typical option to renew provides that if the tenant wants an extension of the term of the lease, and gives notice to that effect not less than 6 months and not more than 12 months from the end of the original lease, then provided the terms of the tenancy have been observed, the landlord will have to grant a new term for the number of years specified in the lease. The option will usually provide that the tenant is to pay the landlord's costs on renewal. It must also be exercised in accordance with its terms: any time limits stated must be adhered to, as must any other formalities required by the option.

Having an option to renew in the lease would clearly be advantageous to a tenant who is buying a new 99 year or shorter lease, but of little importance to a 999 years term. It is a matter for negotiation with the landlord. If no option exists and the lease is running down (for example, 45 years to run), it may be wise to negotiate with the landlord to buy an extension to the term. This may render an otherwise unmarketable lease a saleable item.

options to buy

An option to buy the landlord's freehold is regarded as a separate agreement rather than a term of the lease. The original landlord will remain under the contractual obligation to grant the option and can be sued for damages for breach of contract if he refuses. This is so even if the landlord has sold the freehold. The landlord can avoid this liability by inserting a clause in the lease that the option shall become void unless protected by registration within a specified period. Registration also ensures that a buyer of the freehold is bound by the tenant's rights.

Two issues are usually of importance: who can exercise the option and for how long does it remain open? Much turns on the wording and expression of the clause itself because the option can be exercised only in strict accordance with its terms. The option should therefore deal with the method of exercising it, whether written notice has to be given by the tenant and the time within which it is to be exercised. Normally the option will also state how the price is to be calculated. It is unlikely to be fixed in the original lease. If the machinery or price is not so stated in the lease, the option is likely to be void because of its uncertainty.

The option can be made conditional on the tenant having performed the obligations under the lease.

rights of pre-emption

The landlord may not be prepared to grant the tenant the future right to buy the freehold, but may instead offer the tenant the first refusal if the freehold is to be sold at a future date. The initiative clearly remains with the landlord. When the landlord decides to sell, the tenant will have to be notified and given the opportunity to buy.

The right of pre-emption may provide that the landlord must offer the freehold at a price stated in the lease. The tenant must then decide whether or not to accept the offer. The right, however, may be drafted in such a way as to make the tenant responsible for offering a price, leaving the landlord to decide whether to accept it. In either case, if a contract is not concluded, the landlord will be able to sell the freehold to someone else.

Problems that sometimes arise are that it is unclear when the landlord is supposed to notify the tenant; whether the right exists beyond the first occasion the freehold is offered to the tenant and, in such a case, whether a third party will be bound by it. These points should be spelled out in the lease.

In a time of rising prices, it is unlikely that a right of pre-emption in a modern lease will fix a price. It is not uncommon that the right will be exercisable at 'a price to be agreed upon'. This means that the landlord has to make/accept a bona fide offer reflecting the market value.

protection

If the title to the land is unregistered, the options to buy or to renew will bind a buyer from the landlord only when protected by the entry of an appropriate land charge against the name of the freeholder. It is the tenant who has to make this entry. This needs the appropriate standard form and can be made at the time of the lease being granted, or subsequently.

There is no land charge which can be entered to protect a right of pre-emption (first refusal) – a buyer of the freehold will be bound by this right of the tenant only if he (or his legal adviser) knows about it (or should know about it).

When the title to the land is registered, an option to renew and option to buy can be protected by means of a notice being entered against the freeholder's title. This should be done when the lease is created but can be entered later.

As regards the right of pre-emption (first refusal), the situation is less satisfactory: a right of pre-emption is not registerable. But protection exists while the tenant is in occupation of the flat; the right is protected as an 'overriding interest' so that the buyer from the landlord buys subject to the tenant's rights.

costs

A lease may contain a number of provisions relating to the payment of costs and legal expenses. Options for renewal and for sale may, for example, provide that the tenat has to pay the landlord's legal costs.

the statutory right of first refusal

In addition to and quite separate from acquisition orders (discussed on pages 163/164), another innovation is contained in the Landlord and Tenant Act 1987. This is the right of pre-emption exercisable by tenants when the landlord intends to sell the freehold. Under the Act, the landlord has to offer the right of first refusal to all the tenants. This does not take precedence over the right of pre-emption given to any one individual tenant in his lease.

The essential feature of the statutory right is that the landlord cannot dispose of the premises unless a notice has previously been served on the 'qualifying tenants' offering them the right of first refusal. The Act extends only to certain types of property, benefits a restricted number of tenants and can easily be side-stepped.

to what does the Act apply?

The premises must be a building containing two or more flats held by 'qualifying tenants' who between them hold more than half of the total number of flats in the property. The scheme does not apply, however, where over 50% of the internal floor space of the building is let for non-residential use (for example, shops and offices).

In addition, various landlords are excluded from the Act and these include, most notably, local authorities and housing associations which are governed by other 'right to buy' legislation.

who can buy?

A 'qualifying tenant' is the tenant of a flat who is not exempted from the Act. Those exempted include service and business tenants, for example. The Act does not apply to a tenant who has one lease which covers more than one flat; or has been granted a portion of the common parts or has more than 50% of the total number of flats in the building under various tenancies.

But most of the ordinary residential flat owners would qualify.

when does the right arise?

The right arises when the landlord intends to dispose of the freehold. There are, however, numerous exceptions within which the landlord can dispose of the freehold and not be caught by the scheme (for example, on bankruptcy, marriage settlement, gift to a member of the family or disposal to a charity).

notices and procedure

The procedure is that the landlord must serve notice to the tenants of the proposed sale. The notice must contain particulars of the major terms of the intended transaction, including the price.

The notice constitutes an offer by the landlord to dispose of the property on those terms and this offer may be accepted by the appropriate majority of the tenants. The notice must specify a period of not less than two months for the tenants to respond, and a further period of not less than two months from acceptance, during which the tenants should appoint a person, persons or company to whom the landlord's freehold is to be conveyed.

Once the offer has been accepted, the landlord cannot, during the next three months, dispose of the freehold except to the nominated party. If the tenants fail to nominate a person, the landlord can sell the property, during the subsequent twelve months, to another buyer. Importantly, this sale must not be at a price lower than that offered to the tenants. After 12 months, the whole procedure starts again.

Consideration should be given to the tenants using their management company (or creating one) to act as the nominee. Management companies are considered elsewhere in this book.

disregard of the scheme

Where the landlord sells the freehold to a third party and fails to serve the required notice on the tenants, the new landlord can be required by the appropriate majority of the qualifying tenants to sell to them the freehold he has recently acquired. The tenants must, however, act within certain time limits. They have two months within which to request details of the transaction between the previous and the new landlord, and a further three months to serve a purchase notice on their new landlord.

Any prospective buyer of the freehold would be well advised to ascertain from the tenants whether the seller is free to sell the property. There is procedure for an intending buyer to serve notice on at least 80% of the tenants. Then, unless more than 50% of those tenants serve a notice stating their wish to buy and 28 days have elapsed, he can buy the freehold without fear.

If the flat owners object to the sale of the freehold, their association should serve written notice of their opposition on the prospective buyer and this will ensure that their right of pre-emption can be exercised against the buyer (in the unlikely event that he will wish to continue with his purchase).

WHEN MONEY RUNS OUT

The consequences of mortgage arrears and the failure to pay ground rent are considered in this chapter as are two other unfortunate facts of modern life: debt and bankruptcy, and their potentially devastating effects on the family home.

The last decade has witnessed an economic depression, reminiscent of the 1930's, which is characterised by redundancy and long term unemployment. In spite of this, the dream of home-ownership persists.

Encouragement to buy a home is to be found within the innovation of the 'right to buy' council houses and flats at irresistible discounts and the barely disguised eagerness of institutional lenders to advance money by way of a mortgage.

Many owner-occupiers have been hard hit by the economic recession. In connection with mortgage defaults, the threat to residential security is great: families can become homeless and many have insufficient funds to buy other property in which to live.

charging orders

The Charging Orders Act 1979 permits a creditor, who has obtained a judgment from the High Court or county court, to apply for a 'charging order' as a means of enforcing the judgment debt. This may occur, for example, where a shopper with an in-store credit card has run up a large bill he cannot pay off.

If successful, the creditor is given a charge on the flat and this transforms what was previously a mere debt into an interest in the flat to the benefit of the creditor. The very real threat is that the creditor may than apply to the court for an order of sale and this will often be granted.

The court has a wide discretion whether to make a charging order or not. It is not granted automatically on the request of the creditor. The court also has the power to vary or to discharge the order once made. In exercising this discretion, the court will examine all the circumstances of the case and, in particular, look at the personal details of the debtor (financial, employment and family matters).

The balance must be drawn between the potential hardship to the debtor and family and the interests of the creditor. The 'tug of money' is strong and the courts frequently favour the creditor.

bankruptcy

In bankruptcy the only asset of substantial value, available to satisfy the claims of creditors, is often the family home. The bankrupt's property becomes vested in the trustee in bankruptcy and can be sold to meet the debts.

Where the home is co-owned, however, the trustee has to ask the court for an order for sale. The court, on entertaining such an application, can make such order as it sees fit. Decided cases have shown that the courts tend to favour the trustee in bankruptcy, but it is not inevitable that an order for sale will be granted. The bankrupt's share of the proceeds of sale is then employed to satisfy creditors. The co-owner, unless a surety for a debt, keeps his or her share, untouched by the creditors.

The effects of an order for sale are often catastrophic for the bankrupt, spouse and children and, accordingly, some protection is offered.

the Insolvency Act 1986

This Act instils some compassion into the juggling of the competing interests of the creditor and the family. It achieves this in several, albeit temporary, ways:

○ the bankrupt is offered limited rights of occupation, but only when the flat is also occupied by a person under the age of 18 (for example, a dependent child). This ensures that the bankrupt cannot be evicted from the flat without the authorisation of the bankruptcy court. Before the court can make a possession order, it must take into account the interests of the creditors, the financial resources of the bankrupt, the needs of children and the circumstances of the spouse or cohabitant. The protection is, however, limited because only in exceptional circumstances will a possession order be denied beyond a year after the bankruptcy;

○ the bankrupt's spouse (but not cohabitant) is given certain rights of occupation. Such rights will vicariously benefit the bankrupt. The rights of occupation can be terminated only on the order of the bankruptcy court. The court is referred to certain criteria which it must consider, similar to those mentioned in the previous paragraph. Once more, this protection is only effective for one year following the bankruptcy;

○ where the bankrupt is the co-owner of the flat, the trustee in bankruptcy can apply to the bankruptcy court for an order for sale. The court will take into account the same factors as mentioned above and, again, protection lasts only for one year after bankruptcy.

In such ways, the family home may be preserved, but this is, essentially, only for one year. The Act delays rather than cancels the rights of the creditors and the problem of potential homelessness is merely postponed. During the year the trustee may apply for a charging order to be made.

a ground for eviction

When the landlord ends the contractual relationship between himself and the tenant by forfeiture, the tenant can only be evicted when the landlord has obtained a court order for possession of the flat. Self-help is an unwise course for the landlord to pursue. The Criminal Law Act 1977 makes it a criminal offence for any person to threaten or use violence for the purpose of gaining entry to occupied residential premises. In addition, the Protection from Eviction Act 1977 provides that a landlord who tries to force a tenant to quit the premises (when holding on to possession at the end of a long lease, for example) will commit a further criminal offence. The landlord may also be liable under the civil law for trespass and nuisance, for example.

The Housing Bill 1988 when enacted will strengthen the tenant's position in this respect.

The breach of covenant to pay rent or service charges would be relied on by the landlord as a ground for applying for possession. The court may, on this basis, order the eviction of the tenant.

the mortgage: what can happen on default?

Unless the parties have otherwise agreed, the mortgagee has several standard remedies that can be used against a mortgagor who is in breach of the mortgage agreement.

breach of contract
The lender may sue the borrower for breach of contract to pay the money due. This involves a court action and is only worthwhile if the borrower has the money with which to pay the debt. Most institutional lenders are reluctant to enforce the agreement in this way.

taking possession

The lender has the right to take possession of the mortgaged property from the date of the mortgage even if there is no default. The mortgagee is discouraged from exercising this right unnecessarily by the fact that the lender who takes possession is under an obligation to manage the property prudently. This means that the lender would have to effect reasonable repairs (but at the borrower's cost) and be liable for any negligent or wilful deterioration of the property. In any event, banks and building societies do not wish to occupy mortgaged premises for their own purposes.

In practice, mortgagees take possession only on default and as a means of obtaining vacant possession as a preliminary to exercising their power of sale. A court order for possession will usually be required.

The Administration of Justice Acts 1970 and 1973 give the courts extensive powers to delay or withhold a possession order applied for by the lender. The Act does not apply to mortgages regulated by the Consumer Credit Act.

This provision is designed to give extra time to the borrower who is temporarily in financial difficulties but likely to make up the arrears under the mortgage within a reasonable time. The Administration of Justice Acts do not apply to bank overdrafts secured on the property.

A borrower in financial difficulty can apply to the High Court for a possession order to be postponed. The postponement is unlikely to be for more than 28 days. In this time, the borrower will be expected to make good any arrears.

staving off possession

When the mortgagee wishes to obtain possession of the flat (a necessary preliminary to its sale), the tenant may have several alternatives in which to lessen the chances of the court granting a possession order:

○ raise the necessary money and pay off the mortgage arrears; or
○ request that the building society, bank or other lender accepts a short-term reduction in the monthly repayments; or
○ if possible (not always the case), persuade the lender to allow a switch from an endowment mortgage to a repayment mortgage if the monthly payments are less; this would involve the surrender of the endowment policy and the proceeds can be used to reduce arrears; or
○ with a repayment mortgage, ask for an extension of the term of the mortgage (eg from 25 to 30 years); or
○ the least desirable method, remortgage the flat. This method is emphatically not advised. The risks are great in that the tenant may face higher interest rates, be forced into the grasping hands of the back street credit agencies and end up owing more money than before. The only consolation to this bleak possibility is that it prevents homelessness.

on breakdown of marriage

Where a husband and wife have split up, the spouse who is left in the home has the statutory right to make the mortgage payment. The mortgagee has to accept the payments as if made by the other partner. This will prevent any enforcement action by the lender and may be a means of keeping a roof over the head of the deserted spouse.

When the spouse cannot afford the mortgage repayments and is entitled to benefit from the income support scheme (which has taken the place of supplementary benefit), the mortgage interest may form part of the entitlement of the claimant. It is necessary, however, to show that the mortgagor has left the house and either cannot or will not pay the interest.

forced sale

The lender may be able to sell the property free from the borrower's interest – in practice, that means with vacant possession.

Statute has set up a two stage procedure whereby the remedy arises when instalments are in arrears, but is not exercisable unless and until one of three criteria is satisfied:

○ notice requiring the payment of the mortgage debt has been served on the borrower and default in repayment continues for three months subsequent; or
○ some interest under the mortgage is two months or more in arrears; or
○ there has been a breach of some other provision in the mortgage deed unrelated to the payment of interest or capital (a breach of covenant to insure or repair, for example).

The general rule is that the power of sale is exercisable without needing a court order. However, a court order for possession of the premises will normally be sought by the mortgagee so as to get vacant possession. Once the power of sale has arisen, the buyer from the mortgagee will get good title even where the power of sale has not been exercised correctly.

Any delay in selling the property can affect the borrower adversely. First, the fact that the premises have been vacant for some time often depresses the market value. Second, the borrower is deprived of a home without compensation and third, the interest on the outstanding debt continues to accrue.

The general duty on the lender is to obtain a true market value; building societies are under a more onerous requirement to obtain the best price that can reasonably be negotiated for the property. The proceeds of sale are to be used to clear all mortgage debts, and expenses of sale; any balance left is to be paid to the mortgagor.

receivership

The lender may wish to appoint a receiver in order to enforce the security for the mortgage. This power arises and is exercisable in an identical fashion to the power of sale. The remedy is appropriate where there is income generated from the mortgaged property and the lender does not wish to take possession and sell the property.

foreclosure

The most Draconian measure available to the lender is the remedy of foreclosure. This is the name of the process whereby, on the authority of the court, the title to the property becomes vested in the lender and the borrower is deprived of all interest in the property. The major objection to foreclosure is its unfairness: the power of sale offers a comparatively cheap and simple alternative.

Fortunately, foreclosure is rarely sought and more rarely granted. Although it may appear to offer the lender the opportunity to make a substantial windfall from the borrower's default, foreclosure is unpopular because it is not final: an order can be re-opened by the court at any time, and the court will, generally, substitute an order for sale instead. The process is, therefore, elaborate, uncertain and unjust and is now almost obsolete. Some lenders do still threaten this, however, and it is more worrying for the borrower than a sale order.

COUNCIL FLATS: THE RIGHT TO BUY

The introduction of the public sector 'right to buy' has proved undeniably popular. Well over one million council tenants have now become owner-occupiers. The politics of the concept are that the right ensures the wider spread of wealth through society, encourages the desire to improve and modernise the property, allows an inheritance to be passed to future generations and stimulates independence and self-reliance. Some would retort that, when assessed against the existing background of an urgent need for rented accommodation, the depletion of public housing stock works to the disadvantage of the most needy.

The Housing Act 1985 confers on certain 'secure' tenants the right to buy their house or to take a long leases of their flat for a term of, usually, not less than 125 years and at a ground rent which does not exceed £10 pa. A secure tenant is one who has the benefit of residential security offered by the Act.

who can buy?

The tenant must have been the secure tenant of a public sector landlord (generally a local authority or housing association) for at least two years, or for periods amounting to two years, before the right to buy arises.

The provisions concerning what may constitute the qualifying period are complex, but it is clear that the tenant need not necessarily have lived in one property or have kept to

194 council flats: the right to buy

one landlord. The two years' occupation does not have to be continuous and can be comprised within any period.

A person who, at some stage in the past, had been a secure tenant for the necessary length of time can, therefore, exercise the right to buy when next living in council property.

excluded property

The right to buy extends generally to both houses and flats. Certain kinds of property are, however, excluded. Among the categories of excluded property are any of which the landlord is a charitable housing trust or housing association or is a co-operative housing association. Also outside the right to buy provisions are those houses and flats which have been modified for occupation by physically disabled persons. Nor does the right extend to property which is particularly suitable for occupation by pensioners and has been let in the past to either a pensioner or physically disabled person.

at what price?

The tenant will pay the market value of the property, less any discount. The property is valued at the time the right is exercised. On the grant of a long lease, the valuation is of a flat with vacant possession (that is, disregarding the sitting tenant: the occupier buying the flat) and with a ground rent of £10. The council carries out this valuation, but the tenant has the right to appeal to a district valuer if there is any disagreement.

the discount

The discount available to the prospective buyer depends on the exact number of years the tenant was a secure tenant. Where that period is less than three years, the discount for flats is 44%. When the period exceeds three years, there is an additional discount of 2% for each complete year by which the qualifying period is exceeded. The maximum discount for flats is 70%. It is usually worth waiting an additional year to increase the discount because the date for the valuation will then be later and the price of the property will usually increase more than the greater discount. The discount is subject to a maximum sum which changes from time to time.

the clawback

A person who has bought the long lease in this way and then sells the flat within three years is prevented from making an unjustifiable profit from the transaction. This is achieved by a requirement that all or a percentage of the discount is repaid to the local authority. The amount repayable is the amount by which the market value was originally discounted, less 33.1/3% for each complete year after the grant of the lease.

the mortgage

A secure tenant has the right to a mortgage from the local authority (if finance is not otherwise available). The mortgage is repayable by equal instalments of capital and interest over a period of up to 25 years.

how to exercise the rights

The tenant must serve on the landlord a written notice stating that he wishes to exercise the right to buy. The council has four weeks in which to reply. The council may either accept the tenant's right or deny that the tenant or the property is eligible.

If the right is denied, the tenant must prove eligibility either to the court or to the Secretary of State. If it is accepted, the local authority must serve a notice on the tenant stating: the price; the discount; the provisions to be included in the lease; the right of appeal against valuation; the right to a mortgage; the service charges which are to be payable.

The estimate of service charges (including also repair costs) remains binding on the landlord for the first five years of the lease.

The landlord must also, at the same time, supply the tenant with an application form for a mortgage. The form must be returned completed, generally, within three months. This period may be extended. Following the application for a mortgage, the local authority must reply, as soon as practicable, with yet another notice stating: the amount of the advance proposed; an explanation of how the sum was calculated; the intended provisions of the mortgage deed; the right to a 'shared ownership lease'.

The tenant may apply to have the purchase postponed if sufficient mortgage funds are not made available (the amount proposed may be less than the maximum allowed under the Act). To postpone the transaction, the tenant must pay a returnable deposit of £100 and the purchase price is pegged for the next two years.

shared ownership leases

The right to a shared ownership lease arises where the tenant has established the right to buy, but is not entitled to a full mortgage (of 100%) and has applied for the transaction to be postponed and paid the £100 deposit.

The tenant pays a capital sum to buy a portion (at least 50%) of the lease and has the right to buy successive portions (in blocks of 12.5%) until the entire lease has been acquired. Until the whole lease is bought, the tenant will also pay a rent for the property. If the purchase is assisted by a mortgage advance, the tenant will also be making monthly repayments in respect of the loan.

The tenant will end up with a long lease at a ground rent of less than £10 pa. Until the final portion is acquired, the landlord remains under an obligation to keep the exterior and common parts in repair.

compelling the council to sell

A secure tenant can enforce the rights to buy and obtain a mortgage by going to court. Legal aid may be available and, if successful, the tenant's costs will be met by the local authority. As an alternative route, the tenant can apply to the Secretary of State who has wide ranging powers which include carrying out the sale.

registration

Whether or not the property is in an area where registration of the title is compulsory, all 'right to buy' council purchases are registrable so that the tenant will acquire a registered title to his lease.

FLATS IN SCOTLAND

The law relating to flats in Scotland is very different from that in England and Wales. Leasehold is virtually unknown and since 1974 it has not been possible to grant new leases of residential property for a period of more than 20 years. The overwhelming majority of flats in Scotland are owned on feudal tenure – roughly equivalent to freehold. The rest of this chapter is about feudal tenure flats.

historical introduction

From the middle ages, people in cities tended to build high, partly because space within town walls was limited, but also due to the continental, especially french, style of 'high rise' buildings. Many scottish town buildings were inhabited by all types of people living together; noblemen and the rich at the bottom, merchants and the middle classes in the middle and the poor at the top. The common law long ago evolved a set of rules regulating the rights and duties of the various owners in order to ensure the stability and maintenance of the building.

Feudal tenure originated in Europe in the ninth and tenth centuries and spread to Scotland around 1100. The Crown granted land to important subjects in return for military and other services, these subjects in turn made grants to their followers, and so on. Over the centuries land ownership has spread widely and the services have been changed into payment of money called feuduty. In making a grant of land (a 'feu') the then owner (the 'superior') often imposed conditions on its future use by the person to whom it was granted (the 'feuar'). Typical conditions imposed in granting feus of building plots include the erection of a suitable building, keeping it in good repair, prohibition of further buildings or commercial use of the property. These conditions, called feuing conditions (or real burdens) affect all subsequent owners of the property.

In the past, feuars paid feuduty – an annual fixed sum of money – to their superiors. Creation of new feuduties was prohibited in 1974 and most pre-1974 feuduties have now been redeemed. But, and this is important, even though the feuduty has been redeemed the feuing conditions remain in force.

For all practical purposes, the feuar is the absolute owner of the property so long as he or she observes the feuing conditions. The feuar may sell it, lease it, use it as security for a loan, give it away or leave it by will.

Conditions that affect property can also be imposed without feuing. The owner can simply sell the land subject to conditions and, provided they are incorporated in the title deeds, they affect all subsequent owners of the property.

These conditions and feuing conditions (called collectively 'land obligations') may be modified by the superior or former owner or their successors or by the Lands Tribunal for Scotland.

looking for a flat

The best places to look for property are solicitors' property centres. Most towns and cities in Scotland have 'high street' property centres run by local solicitors where details of property for sale are available. Property marketing in Scotland is mainly done by solicitors. Addresses of property centres are in the telephone directory or you can contact the Law Society of Scotland 26 Drumsheugh Gardens Edinburgh EH3 7YR (telephone 031-226 7411) for a complete list.

Other useful sources are

○ estate agents; these operate in much the same way as estate agents in England and Wales. An agent will send you the details of the properties available locally and some of the larger agents or chains of agents publish regular lists;
○ the scottish national and local newspapers; these carry a vast number of advertisements for flats.

There are plenty of flats in the inner city areas. Blocks of purpose-build flats (often called tenements) although old, are normally solidly constructed of stone. As long as it is in good repair, such property could be a good buy.

Properties are usually advertised at "offers over £X". X is called the 'upset' or asking price. You may have to offer more than the 'upset' but it does depend on the state of the market and how many other people are also wanting to buy the property. Less commonly, properties are marketed at a fixed price. The first person to submit an offer at this price in proper legal form should get it.

It is a good idea to get in touch with a solicitor in Scotland as soon as you start looking for a flat. It is usual to get a solicitor to submit a formal offer on your behalf and as property can be sold very quickly you could miss your dream home while looking around for a solicitor. Early contact also enables your solicitor to explain the procedures and help you get the type of loan best suited to your circumstances. Solicitors have a good knowledge of the local property market and will be able to advise you as to what would be a good buy.

things to consider when buying a flat

Prospective house owners have to think about many aspects of the property such as situation, size, price, condition. Flat buyers have additional concerns. These include

○ the condition of the tenement or block as a whole. There is no point in buying a well maintained flat in a dilapidated tenement
○ liability for repairs. Are they shared? This is especially important for top flat owners
○ maintenance charges. These may be high if contractors do the gardens, clean the stairs and paint the place, or heating or portering is included. You should think very carefully about future maintenance charges when you buy a flat in a large block from the council. Some council blocks built 20 to 30 years ago have turned out to have defects that will be very expensive to remedy
○ getting on with neighbours. As a flat owner you will be sharing facilities with your neighbours and having to deal with them in connection with repairs and other matters of common concern
○ restrictiveness of conditions. For example, you may want to be able to paint your windows and doors any colour you please or keep pets. It would be a mistake to live in a block where these are prohibited.

Banks and building societies are generally not too concerned about what the titles of flats say about repairs and maintenance. This is because the common law rules (which apply if the titles say nothing) are adequate to ensure the block or tenement is reasonably well maintained. Provided the flat you have in mind and the block or tenement in which it is situated are in good repair and structurally stable, you should have no difficulty in getting a loan.

when you find a flat

You should contact your solicitor as soon as you find a flat that you would like to buy. He or she will contact the seller's solicitor or estate agent to have your interest noted. If you have not already got your loan/finance arranged, you should do so at once. Your solicitor will also get the property surveyed for you. A survey is virtually essential as you will not get a loan without one. Even if you are paying cash, you would be extremely foolish to offer for a flat without having had it surveyed beforehand.

The types of survey are similar to those in England and Wales. These are

○ a building society 'survey' which is not much more than a valuation for loan purposes. But you will be given the value placed on the property by the surveyor and a brief outline of its contents and defects
○ a home buyer's survey. This is more thorough and correspondingly more expensive
○ a full structural survey, which is a full survey of the property and all its parts. These cost a lot of money and are rarely used for run of the mill properties.

making an offer

After the survey has been done, you can decide whether or not to go ahead. If you do, your solicitor will put an offer to buy on your behalf; it is better not to attempt submitting an offer yourself. Do not sign any documents without first consulting your solicitor. An offer is a fairly formal document and a binding legal contract exists once it is accepted. It is then too late to alter it if you find out you have not got it right.

Your solicitor's offer is a formal letter (often many pages long) setting out the terms and conditions on which you are willing to buy the flat. It sets out the price, the date of entry (when you take possession even if you do not move in then), the flat you are offering for and all its parts (share of the garden, fixtures and fittings etc) and any extras such as carpets, curtains which are included in the price. There are also conditions to ensure that you get a good legal title, that there are no adverse planning proposals, and that repairs to the block are shared on some reasonably fair basis.

Usually you will not be the only person interested in buying the flat. In this case, sellers fix a 'closing date'. Offers have to be submitted by a certain time on this date, and the seller accepts one of them, although he is not bound to do so. You have to offer blind, as you cannot tell what other people are going to offer. Although your solicitor will advise you, the final decision is yours.

Your solicitor will tell you the fate of your offer an hour or so after the closing time; if you have been successful, a written acceptance of your offer will usually be sent to your solicitor that day.

The acceptance may propose modifications to some of the conditions such as the date of entry, extras, or how repairs are shared. It may take a day or two to resolve all these points and your solicitor will keep you in the picture and ask for your instructions as to how to deal with the proposed modifications. Then a final letter will conclude the contract.

All these letters are known as the 'missives' and are signed by the various solicitors on the clients' behalf; the clients sign nothing at this stage. Once missives have been concluded, you are bound to buy and the seller is bound to sell; there is no gazumping. You do not have to pay a deposit and the price is payable in full on the date of entry.

conveyancing

Once missives have been concluded, your solicitor puts in hand all the procedures necessary to ensure you get a valid title and your building society or bank get a good security for their loan. Various documents are prepared, such as the disposition which transfers the title to you, and the standard security (mortgage deed) which binds you to repay the loan and secures it over the flat. Shortly before the date of entry, you will be sent the standard security to sign. This enables the solicitor to have the loan ready for settlement of the purchase. You will also be asked for a cheque for the balance of the price. Unless you have already sold your previous home or have sufficient ready money, you may need to obtain a bridging loan from your bank.

At settlement, your solicitor will hand over (personally or by post) a cheque for the full price and will receive in return the disposition signed by the seller, the other title deeds to the flat and the keys. The keys will be handed to you, the disposition is recorded in the General Register of Sasines or the Land Register of Scotland, and the other title deeds are sent to the building society or bank that lent you the money. Your solicitor will expect you to pay outlays such as stamp duty and the cost of recording the disposition before or at the settlement, and will send you a bill for his or her fee within a few days afterwards.

whose name on the title?

When two or more people buy a flat together, they have to consider whose name is to go on the title. It is important for the co-owners to discuss this before the title is prepared because it is expensive to put matters right later even if all the co-owners agree.

In Scotland, ownership is almost invariably determined by what the title says. If the disposition is to A, then only A is the owner even though B may have contributed towards the original price, the cost of improvements or repairs or running costs. When the flat is sold, A gets all the money. B may get his or her contributions refunded but is more likely to get nothing. B will never get a share of the property.

In exceptional cases you can be a co-owner even though your name is not on the title. These are when

○ the owner has signed a written document agreeing that you are entitled to the property or a share of it; or
○ the owner swears in court that you are entitled to the home or a share of it; or
○ you prove that your name was omitted by fraud or by error.

These are very uncommon situations and you should not rely on them. To safeguard your contributions, make sure your name goes on the title.

title to two people

Where the title to the flat is in the name of more than one person, each has an equal share unless other proportions are specified. A disposition to A and B gives each a one-half share in the property. Each has a separate and distinct share which he can sell or can be taken to pay his debts. Of course, if the whole property is to be sold, each owner must consent and sign the necessary documents.

Each owner can leave his share by will to any other person or, if there is no will, the share passes under the rules of intestacy to the deceased owner's nearest family. Each owner can also apply to the court for an order that the property be sold and the proceeds divided according to their respective shares. But co-owners can agree that they will not do this and, under the Matrimonial Homes (Family Protection) (Scotland) Act 1981, the court has the power to refuse to order the sale of a matrimonial home owned by a married couple where a sale would be unreasonable.

The title of the co-owners may contain what is called a survivorship destination. The title will say "To A and B (equally between them) and (wholly) to the survivor (of them)". The words in brackets are often inserted but do not add anything. Survivorship destinations are very frequently used by married or co-habiting couples. The only difference a survivorship destination makes is when one of the co-owners (say, A) dies. Then A's share passes automatically to the other co-owner B, unless A is entitled to alter this by will and has made a will referring specifically to the survivorship destination and leaving the share to another person. The rules as to whether A is entitled to alter are complex. However, if, as is usual, both A and B have contributed to the price of the flat, then neither can make a will leaving their share to anybody else.

A survivorship destination may save the expense of making wills if all the couple have is their flat and it cuts down the cost of administering the estate of the first person to die. On the other hand, the couple's wishes may change and, short of divorce, it is impossible to alter a survivorship destination without the agreement of the co-owner. Even if agreement can be reached, a new title has to be prepared and registered in the General Register of Sasines or the Land Register of Scotland and this is not cheap.

matrimonial homes

Scots law gives a spouse who is married to the sole owner the right to occupy the matrimonial home and protects that right in much the same way as the law of England and Wales. But the main differences are

○ the protection is given by the Matrimonial Homes (Family Protection) (Scotland) Act 1981. There is no common law protection
○ the non-owner spouse is entitled to occupy the home with the children
○ the non-owner spouse's rights are not lost if the owner sells the home unless the non-owner spouse agrees or the court dispenses with agreement. This protection is automatic and does not depend on prior registration of any documents in the General Register of Sasines or the Land Register for Scotland
○ on granting a divorce, the courts can continue the rights of the non-owner to occupy the former matrimonial home without altering the ownership of it or, alternatively, they can alter the ownership so as to give the non-owner a share of the home.

Co-habitants also have some protection. However, they are not protected against the sale by the owner and the court can continue the occupancy rights after the relationship breaks down only for a limited period but cannot alter the ownership.

what you own

What parts of the block of flats or tenement each individual proprietor owns depends on the title deeds. Only if the title deeds fail to allocate ownership does the common law apply.

Your solicitor will have noted the provisions of the title deeds when you bought the flat. These notes may be sufficient to settle questions about the ownership of various parts or your liability for repairs. If more details are needed, the titles themselves (or copies) will have to be obtained either from the building society or bank which lent you the money to buy your flat, or from Register House in Edinburgh. The bank or building society will usually send you a photocopy of the titles on request or release them to your solicitor so that they can be inspected and copied. A small charge (about £10) will normally be made.

Copies of all scottish titles are kept at the Registers of Scotland, Meadowbank House, 143 London Road, Edinburgh EH8 7AU (telephone 031-661 6111). These are public registers open to all. You can either write for a copy of the titles of your flat (giving your name, address and the number or location of your flat in the block) or go there and inspect and copy the titles yourself. Either way you will be charged about £10–£20.

Your titles should lay down in some detail what you own. There is no standard style for tenements or blocks of flats; provisions vary according to the date when they were drawn up (modern ones tend to be more detailed) and the part of Scotland you are in (Glasgow, Edinburgh and Aberdeen titles, for example, tend to be slightly different from each other). Nevertheless most styles have certain basic features in common.

A fairly typical style for a block of flats gives each owner not only his or her own flat but also a share in the ground on which the block is built, the surrounding garden ground, the internal passages and stairs, the path up to the front door and drains, pipes and cables so far as these last items are mutual. So if there are 8 flats in your block, you would own a one-eighth share of all these items. A common variation is to make all the external walls shared property as well.

One of the most important parts of a building is the roof. Your titles will usually deal with this in one of two ways. Either the ownership of the roof will be shared between all the flat owners or nothing will be said about who owns the roof but everybody is made liable to maintain it. The difference between these two approaches is explained later.

Your titles may say nothing about who owns what in the block. This is unusual. In this case the common law rules apply. They can be illustrated by looking at a three storey block of flats.

The ground flat owner owns

○ the ground on which the block is built (including the foundations), the surrounding garden ground and boundary walls or fences
○ the external walls of the block from the foundations up to a line half way through the ceiling joists
○ all the internal walls, space etc. enclosed by the external walls.

The middle flat owner owns

○ the external walls from the half way line of the floor joists to the half way line of the ceiling joists
○ all the internal walls, space etc enclosed by the external walls.

The top flat owner owns

○ the external walls from the half way line of the floor joists to the roof
○ the roof and the roof space
○ all the internal walls, space etc enclosed by the external walls.

Most blocks have internal stairs and passages for reaching the various flats. These together with the bit of the roof over the stairs are shared by all those people whose property they form an access to. Each section of the walls enclosing the stairs and passages is shared between the person who owns the flat on the other side and all those sharing the ownership of the stairs or passage in question.

A chimney head is not regarded as part of the roof. It is owned by the flat owners having vents in it, in proportion to the number of vents each has. Each chimney pot on the other hand is the property of the person whose vent it sits on.

Downpipes from the rhones (the word means roof gutters) to the drain are owned in sections; each proprietor of a flat owns that part of the pipe running down his or her external walls. Each proprietor also owns the portions of any drains, water or gas pipes or cables passing through his or her property.

Although it is unusual for the titles to be completely silent about ownership, they quite often omit some items. If so, the common law applies. For example, the titles may share the ownership of the roof but say nothing about the chimney heads. In this case the chimney heads are owned by those having vents in them.

what you can and cannot do

Major alterations or extensions to a building require planning and building control permission. Even minor structural work needs the latter. Permission should be obtained before work is started, otherwise you may find yourself having to restore the building to its original condition as well as paying for the abortive work. Your local authority planning and building control departments will advise you about the need for permission and the sort of work that is likely to be approved. The remainder of this section assumes that any necessary planning and building control permissions have been obtained.

common law

Even when your proposed work is to be carried out entirely to your own flat or other parts that you own, the law lays certain restrictions on you in the interests of all the other owners in the block. Any other owner can stop you from doing anything which is injurious to the structure of the block, such as knocking down an internal load-bearing wall or adding an extra storey to your top flat. This is done by applying to the court for an order called an interdict. If you carry on after having been interdicted, you are in contempt of court and may be fined or imprisoned as well as having to restore the building. If your neighbours apply for an inter-dict, it is up to you to satisfy the court that your proposed work is perfectly safe. Non-structural alterations which are out of keeping with the rest of the block or district may be prohibited under the titles. If not, and planning permission has been granted, there is not much objectors can do about it.

When you own property along with other people in the block (a chimney head, for example), first, all the owners must agree before any kind of work is done on it, and secondly, any of the others in the block can object on the ground that the work would be injurious to the structure of the block. Essential repairs are an exception, any owner can do these without getting consent. But often a better way of getting essential repairs done is via the local authority.

You may be thinking of enlarging your top flat by a roof extension. What consents you need from your neighbours depends on your titles. Many titles give all the owners in the block an equal share of the roof. In this case you can do nothing without all their consents. Their refusal to consent cannot be overridden, however unreasonable you may think they are. You will have to buy their consent or abandon the project. On the other hand, your titles may say nothing about ownership of the roof so that under the common law you are the sole owner. Your neighbours can object only if your work will damage the structure or you plan to extend beyond the existing roof-line.

prohibitions in title

Quite apart from the above rules, your titles will almost certainly contain additional prohibitions. The more modern a block you live in, the longer the list of things you may be prohibited from doing. Typical prohibitions are no additional building to be erected, no alterations, no subdivision of flats, and no commercial use. In a modern block you may also be forbidden to keep pets, put in gas, deviate from the exterior paintwork scheme, hang clothes in the garden or park cars overnight in front of the block. Remember it does not matter how long ago the prohibitions were created, they are still binding on you (unless they are varied or discharged).

If your proposed works are in breach of the conditions in your title you will have to get permission from the superior or other person or their successors (superior for short) who imposed the conditions.

For minor alterations such as adding railings to the boundary wall, a simple letter of consent from the superior or the superior's solicitors is sufficient. No charge is usually made for this. But where the proposed works require a major change in the condition, turning the ground floor flat into a shop or dentist's surgery for example, a more formal document called a Minute of Waiver is called for. You will have to pay the superior's legal expenses for having this document prepared and many superiors will demand a capital payment as well.

If the superior refuses permission or demands too great a capital payment, you could apply to the Lands Tribunal for Scotland, 1 Grosvenor Crescent, Edinburgh EH12 5ER (telephone 031-225 7996) to have the conditions of your title varied or discharged. A leaflet on conditions and how they may be varied or discharged is obtainable from the Lands Tribunal. You will need a solicitor's help in making an application. Legal aid is available.

Sometimes the superior has no objection to your proposed breach of your title conditions, but the neighbours are up in arms. Whether they can stop you depends on the titles. Some titles give the neighbours an express right to enforce the title conditions, but the right can sometimes also be implied from the terms of the titles. The law here is complex and uncertain and you should seek legal advice. If your neighbours are entitled to object, you will either have to modify or abandon your proposals, buy their consent or apply to the Lands Tribunal to have the condition in question varied or discharged.

getting repairs and maintenance done

Repairs and maintenance cause more ill-feeling amongst flat owners than almost anything else. It is bad enough having to pay to maintain your own flat, but it is much worse having to pay for other people's property (ground flat owners having to pay for the roof or lift, for example). The three commonest ways of organising repairs and maintenance are described below.

Many titles simply oblige the flat owners 'to maintain the block' or some similar phrase. This adds little to the common law. Necessary repairs must be carried out and if some owners refuse or will not allow contractors access, an application to the court is required. Asking the local authority to exercise its statutory powers is simpler and cheaper.

Owners cannot be compelled to do anything other than necessary repairs. They can, for instance, let the paint flake off their windows however much this spoils the appearance of the block. An appeal to self-interest or possible liability for damage to other flats may work, but you should not harass neighbours about inessential repairs. They may be less well off than you or are only going to stay for a short time and are therefore not interested in long-term maintenance.

The difficulty of getting the agreement of all the flat owners, especially in large blocks or where some owners are absentee landlords, has led to the gradual deterioration of many old blocks. One solution, common in Glasgow and the west, is for the titles to provide that a specified proportion (such as three-quarters or a majority) of the owners are entitled to instruct repairs on behalf of all. Provided the requisite number of owners agree, the others are bound to pay their share of the cost. A modern variant is for a resident's association to be formed and for the decisions of the association taken in accordance with its constitution to be binding on all the residents. A court order, or going via the local authority, still has to be resorted to if an owner refuses access.

The titles may provide for a factor to organise the repairs and maintenance. Factoring was common in the west and is being used more and more in large modern developments. The factor is usually a surveyor, estate agent or architect appointed initially by the developer (or the flat owners can get together and appoint a factor). In a good working relationship, the factor will consult about major repairs (such as replacement of the lift) but not about routine maintenance.

The titles of many factored blocks contain fairly explicit maintenance programmes. For example, the lawns have to be cut regularly, the exterior repainted every 3 years and the lift serviced annually. Each owner will receive a regular (usually half yearly) bill for the work carried out since the last bill. The major grumbles about factoring are the expense (since the factor has to be paid), lack of consultation, and inability to get the work done to a proper standard as the owners may be given little say in the choice of contractors. In the last resort, unless the title deeds forbid this, the owners can dismiss the factor and either do without – or appoint another of their own choice.

sharing the cost

Under the common law, you are liable to pay only for the repair and maintenance of the portions of the block that you own or share in. So, for example, the ground and middle flat owners are not liable for roof repairs, while the top and middle flats are not liable for garden maintenance or underpinning defective foundations. Middle flats come off best. In fact, they are better all round; the rain doesn't come in on you when the roof leaks, you have a good view and are less likely to be burgled.

In most cases, the titles rather than the common law say how the costs are to be shared. A typical scheme is for all the owners in the block to share the costs of repairs to the roof, rhones, chimney heads, downpipes, common stairs and

passages, all mutual pipes, drains and cables and garden
maintenance. Sometimes each owner pays an equal share,
sometimes the share is in proportion to each flat's feuduty
or rateable value (R.V.).

Example: Roof bill of £1200.

	Equal Shares	Feuduty	Rateable Value
Top flat feuduty £3 R.V. 500	£400	£300	£600
Middle flat feuduty £4.50 R.V. 250	£400	£450	£300
Ground flat feuduty £4.50 R.V. 250	£400	£450	£300

You are bound to pay only if your title (or the common
law) says you must or you have agreed to pay. What your
neighbours have in their titles is beside the point. This gives
rise to a nasty trap for top flat owners where those
responsible for preparing the titles did not put an obligation
to share the roof costs in all the other titles. Under the
common law rules which apply when the titles are silent, as
top flat owner you are liable for the whole cost of roof repairs
but although your title says everyone is to share, you can
recover a share only from those owners whose titles contain
an obligation to pay. It can turn out that you have to pay
most or all of the cost yourself. To avoid this trap your
solicitor should, when buying the flat, examine the titles of
every other owner in the block as well as yours.

Apart from your neighbours paying a share (or you being
able to increase your mortgage), sources of finance to meet

your repairs and maintenance costs are

○ a local authority repair grant. Enquire at your district (or islands) council housing department

○ your buildings insurance policy. It will not cover making good ordinary wear and tear but a portion of the work needed may be due to something (such as a burst pipe) covered by the policy

○ a guarantee. Some contractors (dry rot eradicators or roofers for example) guarantee their work for a certain number of years. Contact the firm if trouble occurs in an area previously treated

○ the previous owner. It may have been part of your bargain with the previous owner when you bought the flat that he or she would remain liable for repairs called for under local authority notices issued before you agreed to buy. Check with your solicitor

○ a negligence claim. If another owner knew about a defect in his property which was likely to cause damage to your flat and failed to do anything about the defect, the other owner is liable for the damage. See your solicitor if you think you have a claim.

You should never sign a contract or order repair work to be done to the block on your own. If you do, you will have to pay the contractor and you may find it difficult to get your neighbours to pay their shares. A contract for a shared repair should be signed by all those owners involved. The contractor will share out the cost between all the owners according to their liability under the titles if advised what that is.

For urgent repairs, where there is not time to get all the owners to agree to pay, you should get in touch with your district council. They can take emergency action and apportion the bill.

local authority repairs

The local authority (district or islands council) has powers under the Civic Government (Scotland) Act 1982 and the Housing (Scotland) Act 1987 to require flat owners to rectify defects in the block in order to bring it into a reasonable state of repair. In assessing what is reasonable, the council will look at the age, character and location of the building.

Asking the council to exercise its powers has advantages but also disadvantages. When you contact the council's housing department, an official will come out to inspect the building. Emergency repairs such as making good a crumbling chimney head will be done at once. For non-emergency repairs, a statutory repairs notice is issued to all the owners calling on them to carry out the specified repairs within a certain time limit.

The advantages of contacting the council are that

○ the property is inspected by an impartial skilled person who is not trying to obtain work
○ it is easier to convince reluctant neighbours that repairs are necessary
○ you are more likely to get a repairs grant from the council.

But

○ the council inspector may require more repairs to be done than you anticipated. For example, while on the roof he may see the chimney heads need repointing
○ the work may be required to be done to a higher standard than you want. This is especially true for grant-aided work.

The service of a statutory repairs notice should ensure that the owners get together to get estimates, select a contractor and get the work done. Expensive repairs are best supervised by an architect or surveyor. If the owners fail to get the repairs done, the council will step in the carry them out itself, although it usually needs a request or pressure from one or more of the owners to get it to do this. Where the council does the work itself, it can share out the cost among the owners as it pleases. In Edinburgh, the shares are always in proportion to the rateable value of each owner's flat.

Sometimes it is better to let the council do the work. It does not need the consent of all the owners. So, if some of your neighbours cannot be contacted or are uncooperative, get the work done by the council. Another advantage is that the council will do the often unpleasant task of getting people to pay.

But there are disadvantages. First, about 10% is added for administration and supervision of the work. Secondly, the owners have no control over the work. Thirdly, the way the council shares out the total cost may not be in accordance with the titles, so that the owners have to settle up amongst themselves later. This can cause a lot of ill-feeling since many owners do not understand the reason for the adjustments.

You would be well advised to contact the council in the case of an emergency repair. If you contact a firm yourself, you are liable for the bill and you may find it difficult to get the other owners were not contacted beforehand to pay their share.

insurance

Nearly all home owners have insurance to cover damage to, or destruction of, their property. In the case of a flat, your insurance policy should cover not only your flat but also all the other parts of the block you are liable to maintain.

Problems can arise if each owner arranges insurance individually. Some may insure for too little or forget to renew their policy. Some policies may not cover the accident which has happened. Extensive repairs needed following a good fire or discovery of dry rot sometimes cannot be done because certain owners cannot afford to pay.

Most of these problems can be avoided by having a good common insurance policy covering the whole block with each person paying a share of the premium. It is difficult to have a common policy unless the block has a residents' association or a factor because otherwise one of the owners has to get the others to agree, arrange the policy and collect the shares of the premium. Banks or building societies will accept a common policy instead of an individual policy as long as it is with a reputable company and covers all the normal risks.

Whatever kind of policy you have, it is essential that the property is insured for its reinstatement value (what it would cost to rebuild it) not its market value (what it would sell for). For flats in old stone built blocks, the reinstatement value is often two or three times the market value. Failure to insure for full reinstatement value may mean the insurance company may pay only a part of your claim or may refuse to pay anything.

council flats

Many people have taken advantage of the right-to-buy in the Tenants' Rights Etc. (Scotland) Act 1980 (now the Housing (Scotland) Act 1987) and bought the home which they rented from the council. If you have bought your flat in a large council block, your title will bind you to pay your share of the repairs to the block. But since most of the other flats are still owned by the council you will have virtually no say in how the block is run or maintained. It is extremely difficult for you to get them to do a repair you consider necessary (you can hardly use the local authority procedure, since the council housing department will not tell the same department to do something they don't want to do), or prevent them doing expensive upgrading.

Unfortunately, some post-war council blocks built suffer from inherent structural defects which are extremely expensive or impossible to rectify. Your share of the costs could quite easily cost more than you paid for your flat, or your flat, although sound, may be unsaleable. For certain buildings which are known to be liable to contain such defects, you can require the council to buy back the flat under the Housing Defects Act 1984. You should seek help from a housing advice agency or your solicitor.

debt and bankruptcy

The Charging Orders Act 1979 does not apply. A creditor who has got a decree against the debtor can apply to the Court of Sessions for an adjudication of the debtor's flat. This will be granted almost automatically and enables the creditor to evict the debtor and let the flat to tenants. The creditor cannot sell, however, until a period of ten years has elapsed without payment of the debt and then only by going to court for an order making the creditor the owner. Adjudications are very rarely used.

bankruptcy

The Bankruptcy (Scotland) Act 1985 protects the rights of the bankrupt's family to the family home, but only for a year.

When the bankrupt's (ex) spouse is living in the home, the trustee can sell only if the (ex) spouse consents or an order is obtained from the court. Where the bankrupt lives there with a child of the family but no spouse, the bankrupt must consent unless a court order is obtained. The child includes a step-child, a child accepted into the family, and grown up children: there is no age limit. Co-habitants are not protected unless there is a child living in the home.

In deciding whether to order a sale, the courts must take into account the financial position of the (ex) spouse and any children, the creditors' interests in having their debts paid, and how long the home was used as a family home before bankruptcy.

selling your flat

There are three main ways in which to sell your flat:

○ yourself
○ through a solicitor
○ through an estate agent.

Doing it all yourself is not recommended. Most people ask a solicitor to handle the sale, especially the final stages of the closing date and accepting formal offers. Solicitors' fees are about 1/2% to 1% of the selling price, plus the cost of advertisements and other outlays. For this, your solicitor will prepare the advertisements and advertise the flat in the newspapers, weekly lists of property being sold by local solicitors and the local property centre, advise you on the price and handle all the enquiries and negotiations leading to the conclusion of the missives. You will be expected to show prospective buyers around the flat, the solicitor will charge more if he or she has to do this as well. Legal fees for conveyancing will be in addition to the selling fee, although many solicitors will quote an inclusive fee.

Estate agents' charges and ways of operating are much the same as in England and Wales. Agents will hand over the formal offer to purchase to your solicitor, or advise buyers to send them directly to the solicitor. You will have to pay your solicitor's usual conveyancing fees as well as the agents' commission.

Whether you are going to use your solicitor or an agent, it is a good idea to see your solicitor as soon as you decide to sell. Your solicitor will then get the title deeds from the building society or bank, order certificates from the district and regional councils relating to planning, repair notices and other matters. He or she will thus be in a position to deal with the enquiries and offers from prospective purchasers' solicitors.

If you own the flat along with another person, he or she must consent to its sale. A sole owner who is married must, under the Matrimonial Homes (Family Protection) (Scotland) Act 1981, obtain the spouse's consent. Failure to obtain your spouse's consent will mean the purchaser will withdraw leaving you with a large bill and possibly also a claim for damages.

after the advertisement

After people have come to see your flat, hopefully your solicitor or agent should receive calls from the solicitors of possible buyers noting their client's interest. Everyone who has noted an interest should be given the chance to put in an offer. You will know that you have someone really interested when a surveyor comes to survey the flat.

You can agree a price orally (this is not binding until it is in writing) but then you should tell the purchaser to submit a formal offer to your solicitor. Do not under any circumstances sign an agreement without consulting your solicitor.

There may be a lot of interest in your flat. In this situation, your solicitor or agent will advise you to set a closing date – a date by which formal offers to buy must be submitted. You usually get a better price this way than accepting the first reasonable offer. On the other hand, it is more of a cliff hanger. With luck, several offers will be submitted on the closing date. Your solicitor will contact you and advise you which (if any) to accept. Usually the highest offer is chosen but personal considerations, the proposed date of entry or the extras including in the price may lead to a different choice. Your solicitor can negotiate on things like the date of entry and the extras, but it is not usual to try and get a better price.

Your solicitor will send a written acceptance of the offer at once to the successful offerer's solicitor. However, there usually has to be a further exchange of correspondence adjusting all the details, but this should not last for more than a day or so. The offer and the letters following on it are called the missives and constitute the contract. Your solicitor will act on your behalf so that you do not have to sign anything at this stage. Once the missives are concluded, you are bound to sell and the purchaser is bound to buy; there is no gazumping.

conveyancing and settlements

Once missives have been concluded, your solicitor will send the titles to the buyer's solicitor who prepares the document transferring title (called the disposition). Your solicitor will make sure the disposition is correct, answer queries from the buyer's solicitor and arrange to pay off the building society or bank loan and discharge the security.

A few days before the agreed date of entry (when the buyer is to take possession), your solicitor will send you the disposition to sign and will remind you that the keys have to be made available. You can hand over the keys to the buyer yourself but it is best to give them to your solicitor in case there are any last minute hitches.

On the date of entry, your solicitor hands over the disposition, the other title deeds of the flat and the keys to the buyer's solicitor and receives in exchange a cheque for the full purchase price. After deducting any outstanding building society or bank loan and his fees and outlays, your solicitor should hand over the balance of the price to you that day or the next day.

GLOSSARY

advance
the mortgage loan

assignment
the sale of a tenant's lease to another person

beneficial ownership
having the use or benefit of a property without owning its legal title
see also equitable interest

charge
any right or interest, subject to which a property may be owned, especially a mortgage; also used to denote a debt, or a claim for payment

charge certificate
when there is a mortgage, the certificate issued by the Land Registry to the mortgagee of a property which has a registered title
see also land certificate

charges register
one of the three parts which make up the register at the land registry of a property with a registered title; contains details of restrictive covenants, mortgages and other interests, subject to which the registered proprietor owns the property

chattel
any moveable possession

civil law
that part of the law which confers rights and imposes duties on individuals and deals with resolving disputes between them. Most of the actions between landlord and tenants are matters of civil law

common law
that part of the law which is derived not from statutes but from the principles and the precedents set by earlier decisions of the court

completion
the final stage of the legal transaction when buying or selling the long lease of a flat

contract
any legally binding agreement; on the sale of a property it is the document, in two identical parts, one signed by the buyer and the other by the seller, which, when the parts are exchanged, commits both the buyer and the seller to complete the transaction by transferring ownership in exchange for paying the purchase money

conveyancing
the legal and administrative process of transferring the ownership of land or any buildings on it, or a part of a building (such as a flat), from one owner to another

county court
court which deals with small civil cases, including landlord and tenant matters (generally, the amount at stake must not be more than £5000)

covenant
an undertaking between landlord and tenant whereby they
are bound to do certain things (such as to pay the rent or to
repair) or to abstain from doing (such as misuse property);
may be expressed (that is, set out in the lease), or implied

criminal law
the part of the law which punishes behaviour harmful to the
community as a whole, as against the civil law which
confers rights and duties on individual people

dealings
any transaction involving property

deed
a legal document which, instead of being merely signed, is
'signed, sealed and delivered'; the transfer of the legal title
to leasehold property has to be by deed

demised premises
property which is the subject matter of a lease with certain
implied covenants, such as promising that the tenant shall
have quiet enjoyment of the premises

deposit
part of the purchase price, usually 10%, which the buyer has
to pay at the time of exchange of contracts. It can be forfeited
to the seller if the buyer withdraws (through no fault on the
part of the seller) after signing a binding contract

easement
the legal right of a property owner to use the facilities of
another's land – for example, a right of way

endowment mortgage
a loan on which only the interest is paid throughout the term and which is paid off at the end with the proceeds of an endowment insurance policy which is assigned to or deposited with the lender as additional security for the loan

enfranchisement
tenant with long lease buying the freehold of the property under the Leasehold Reform Act 1967

enquiries before contract
a set of detailed questions about many aspects of a property which the seller, or his legal adviser, is generally asked to answer before the buyer is prepared to sign a contract; also called preliminary enquiries

enquiries of local authority
a number of questions asked of a local authority on a printed form about a particular property; the form is usually sent with, and loosely speaking forms part of, the buyer's local search which is made before contracts are exchanged

equitable interest
rights in a property which fall short of legal title, for example where a lease is not properly created by deed it may be an equitable lease; also used to describe the interest of beneficial ownership when this is not the same as the legal title

estate
person's interest in land (may be freehold or leasehold)

exchange of contracts
the stage at which the buyer has signed one copy of the

contract and sent it to the seller, and the seller has done the same in return, so that both become legally bound to go through with the transaction

fixtures
articles which, being attached (by screws, concrete or pipes, for instance) to the property itself are presumed to have become legally part of the property so that they are included in a sale, unless specifically excluded by the contract

foreclosure
the mortgagee's remedy whereby he obtains the property rather than repayment of the loan and keeps the money already repaid; needs a court order

forfeiture
the means by which a landlord can bring a lease to an early end following a breach of covenant by the tenant

freehold
the absolute ownership of property until the end of time as opposed to leasehold

grant
formal giving or transferring, for example of a lease

ground rent
small sum payable periodically to the landlord (the free-holder or ground owner) by tenant who holds leasehold property on a long lease

interest in land
a right to, stake in, or any form of ownership of, property such as a flat

joint tenants
two (or more) people who hold property as co-owners;
when one dies, the whole property automatically passes to
the survivor(s) (this is in contrast with what happens in the
case of tenants-in-common)

land certificate
the certificate issued to the registered proprietor of a
property which has a registered title, showing what is
entered on the register of that property at the Land Registry.
When the property is mortgaged, no land certificate is
issued (it is retained at the Land Registry) and instead a
charge certificate is issued to the mortgagee

Land Charges Department
a government department in Plymouth where rights over,
and interests in, unregistered property are recorded;
charges are registered against the name of the owner, not
the property concerned

landlord
the owner of property who grants a lease or sublease of the
property (word is interchangeable with lessor)

Land Registry
a government department (head office in London and
district registries in various other places in England and
Wales) where details of properties with a registered title are
recorded

leasehold
ownership of property for a fixed number of years granted
by a lease which sets out the obligations of the leaseholder,
for example regarding payment of rent to the landlord,

repairs and insurance; as opposed to freehold property, where ownership is absolute

legal charge
a mortgage, especially one framed so as to include the words 'legal charge'

lessee
the person to whom a lease was originally granted, and, more commonly, the present leaseholder (word is inter-changeable with tenant)

lessor
the person who originally granted a lease; also, the present landlord

local land charges register
a register kept by the local authority, containing charges of a public nature affecting the property, which is consulted when a local search is made

local search
an application made on a duplicate form, to the local authority for a certificate providing certain information about a property in the area. Also denotes the search certificate itself. Loosely speaking, a local search also includes the answers given by the local authority to a number of standard enquiries, made on another special form

mortgage
loan for which a property is the security. It gives to the lender (mortgagee) certain rights in the property, including the power to sell if the mortgage payments are not made

mortgage deed
the document setting out the mortgage conditions

mortgagee
one who lends money on mortgage, such as a building society, bank, local authority, insurance company or private lender

mortgagor
the borrower (whose property is security for the loan)

negligence
breach of a legal rule which imposes a duty of care on any person who ought to foresee that his/her act or omission could cause loss or injury to another

official search
an application to an official authority (such as a local authority, the Land Registry or the Land Charges Registry), to find out some relevant facts about a particular property

overriding interests
rights which are enforceable against a property, even though they are not referred to on the register of the property at the Land Registry

possession action
exercising the powers or controls of ownership; procedure whereby a landlord goes to the court to evict a tenant or other lawful residential occupier

preliminary enquiries
enquiries before contract

premium
capital sum (the purchase price) paid for a long lease; also
the payments to insurers for insurance cover

re-entry
landlord lawfully retaking possession of a property with a
court order on forfeiture

register
in the case of a property with a registered title, the record for
that property kept at the Land Registry, divided into the
property, the proprietorship and the charges registers

registered title
title or ownership of freehold or leasehold property which
has been registered at the Land Registry, with the result that
ownership is guaranteed by the state; in many parts of the
country, registration of title is compulsory

relief
redress, remedial action, sanctioned by law, for example
where the tenant's lease is allowed by the court to continue
despite the fact that the landlord has obtained a judgment
for forfeiture

remedy
legal redress

repayment mortgage
loan on which part of the capital as well as interest is paid
back by regular instalments throughout the term of the loan

reservations
rights set out in a lease as being kept by the landord over the

property he has let; the converse of easements and usually of similar nature

reserved property
parts of the building or garden which the landlord keeps under his control

residential occupier
someone who lives in the property as his home

reversion
an interest in property which will eventually return to the original owner (or his successors) when the time during which another person holds the property comes to an end; loosely used to denote the freehold

search
an enquiry for, or an inspection of, information recorded by some official body, such as a local authority, the Land Registry or the Land Charges Department

secure tenant
an individual who occupies as his only or principal home a property of which the landlord is a local authority, or a county council, or a housing association or one of a few other public sector landlords

security of tenure
the right to remain in possession after the original contract has expired

stamp duty
a tax payable to the government on some deeds and documents, including deeds of transfer, conveyance or

assignment of property at a price above (at present) £30,000; deeds and documents cannot be used as evidence or registered at the Land Registry unless they are properly stamped

statute
an act of parliament

statutory
a right or obligation arising from a statute or subordinate legislation made under it

subject to contract
provisionally agreed, but not so as to constitute a binding legal contract; either the buyer or the seller may still back out with no legal consequences, without giving any reason

sublease
a lease carved out of another lease, necessarily for a shorter period, created by a person who has only a leasehold interest in the property

subtenant
tenant who leases property from a landlord who owns a leasehold, not a freehold interest in that property. It is possible for a chain of tenancies to be built up running from the freeholder (the head-landlord) to his tenant and down to a subtenant, then to a sub-subtenant, and so on. Each tenant becomes the landlord of his own subtenant down to the last link in the chain – the tenant in actual occupation

superior landlord
someone with a higher interest than the tenant's immediate landlord; if A, a freeholder, grants a 99 year lease to B, and B then grants a 21 year lease to C, the superior landlord is A

tenant
the person to whom a lease is granted (word is interchangeable with lessee)

tenants in common
two (or more) people who together hold property in such a way that, when one dies, his share does not pass automatically to the survivor but forms part of his own property and passes under his will or intestacy (this is in contrast with what happens in the case of joint tenants)

'time is of the essence'
making it a term of the contract that stated time limits must be observed; if a party is late in performing a contractual obligation where time is of the essence, the other party is released from his corresponding contractual obligation. Completion time can be made 'of the essence' in a contract for the sale of land by either party serving a 'notice to complete'

title
ownership of a property

title deeds
documents going back over 15 years or longer which prove the ownership of unregistered property

transfer
a deed which transfers the ownership of a property, the title to which is registered at the Land Registry (as opposed to the deed used where the title is unregistered, which is a conveyance in the case of a freehold, and an assignment in the case of a leasehold)

trustee
a person in whom the legal ownership of property is vested, but who holds it for the benefit of someone else (called a beneficiary)

trustees for sale
people who hold property as trustees on condition that they should sell the property, but usually with a power to postpone doing so indefinitely if they want to

unregistered land
property, the title or ownership of which has not been registered at the Land Registry

vendor
the seller

INDEX

abatement notice, 146
abstract of title, 28
accountant, 116, 118
acquisition order, 163, 164
action area, 158
action for damages, 131
adjacent flats, 12, 152
adjoining property, 140, 152
Administration of Justice Acts
  1970 and 1973, 188
advancement, 108
advertisements for flats, 200, 222
agent for the seller, 31, 32
alterations, 88
annoyance, causing, 173
applying to court, 22, 173. 197, 205
appointment of manager, 161
apportionment of service charge,
  115, 116, 117, 121
arrears, paying off, 135
articles of association, 127
attachment of earnings order, 133
auditor, 129
authorisation of court, 175

bankruptcy, 182, 184, 185
– court, 186
– in Scotland, 221 et seq.
Bankruptcy (Scotland) Act 1985,
  221
banks, 35, 36, 188, 201
binding contract, 25, 202, 224
boundary walls, 17, 209
breach of contract, 30, 48, 50, 52,
  75, 76, 188
breach of covenant, 67, 72 et seq.,
  134, 169, 187
breach of duty, 78, 82
breakdown of marriage, 96, 103
bridging loan, 31, 204

builders, 82
building societies, 35 et seq., 188
buying a flat together, 94 et seq.
buying from co-owners, 109

certificate of recognition, 124
chain of indemnities, 71, 74
chain of transactions, 25, 31
charge certificate, 34, 44, gl.
charge on the property, 102, 112
charging order, 184, 185
Charging Order Act 1979, 184
chattel, 24, gl.
children, 99, 101, 103, 108, 149,
  150, 173, 186, 222
citizens advice bureau, 139
Civic Government (Scotland) Act
  1982, 218
class F land charge, 102
closing date, 203, 204
cohabitants, 95, 207, 222
co-owned flat, selling, 98, 99
co-owners, 94, 108
– and proceeds of sale, 97, 98
– and trust for sale, 97
– disputes, 98, 99
– not living in flat, 111
– Scotland, 204 et seq.
co-ownership, 97, 106
– and bankruptcy, 185, 186
co-purchaser, 37, 43
commercial use, 199
common intention, 107
common law, 141, 201, 207, 209,
  210, 211, gl.
– Scotland, 201, 207, 209, 210,
  211, 214, 215, 216
common parts, 16, 18, 65, 125
– grant, 160
completion, 15, 33, 47, gl.

compulsory improvement, 157
compulsory purchase, 156, 157,
   161, 163, 175
– of landlord's freehold, 163
concurrent lease, 125, 128
conflict of interests, 15
consent for assigning, 66
– for subletting, 41
– of landlord, 64
consequential loss, 138
constructive trust, 105, 108
Consumer Credit Act 1974, 42, 43,
   188
contempt of court, 149
contract, 22 *et seq.*
– races, 20, 21
– standard form of, 22
– unenforceable, 15, 22, 224
contribution, to deposit, 106, 107
– to houshold expenses, 106, 205
– to legal expenses, 106, 107
– to mortgage payments, 106, 111
– to purchase price, 111, 206
Control of Pollution Act 1974, 146
conveyancers, 15, 46, 75
conveyancing fees, 106, 223
conveyancing, Scotland, 204
council blocks, Scotland, 201, 221
council tenants, 44, 193
county court, 83, 134, 155, 161,
   164, gl.
court action, 8, 75, 116, 117, 122,
   188
court, allowing tenant to stay on,
   173
court, applying to, 142, 143, 164
court order, 101, 118, 155, 191
– for mortgage default, 36, 188
court's discretion, 30, 99, 101, 132,
   136, 137, 146, 155, 162, 164, 185,
   192, 222
covenant, 7, 10, 17, 46, 54, 58, 62,
   64, 67, 84 *et seq.*, 168, gl.
– enforcing, 13, 68, 70, 131 *et seq.*
– negative, 84

– positive, 84
– remaining liable for, 126, 128,
   130
– to pay service charge, 114
– to repair, 86, 90
creating a trust, 96
Criminal Law Act 1977, 187
criminal offence, 146, 175, 187
criminal proceedings, 175
cross claim, 138

date of entry, 203, 224, 225
date of expiry, 168
death, 95, 206
debt, 184, 185
– in Scotland, 221 *et seq.*
decorating the exterior, 116, 208
decree absolute, 101
deed, 54, 170
– to create lease, 11
Defective Premises Act 1972, 81,
   145, 151
deposit, 22, 30, 46, 106, 130, 196,
   gl.
– amount of, 23
– and chains, 31, 33
– claiming back, 29
– forfeiting, 21, 32
– guarantee schemes, 32
– less than 10%, 30, 31
– pre-contract, 21
– recovery of, 30, 50
– repaying, 30, 32, 51
– Scotland, 203
derogation from grant, 92, 93
dilapidation, 155, 171
direct management, 125
directors, 127, 129
discretionary remedy, 49, 51, 132
disposition, 204, 225
disrepair, 143, 154, 156
distress, 133, 134, 137
divorce, 96, 102, 103, 206
do-it-yourself conveyancing, 16
dog destruction order, 149

dogs and cats, 90, 149, 201, 212
draft contract, 21, 46
draft lease, 54
drip mortgages, 45
duty of care, 76, 80, 142, 150

easements, 60, gl.
economic loss, 81
emergency repairs, 218, 219
end of lease, 64, 91, 134, 168 *et seq.*, 171
– and repairs, 91, 171
ending lease prematurely, 169
endowment mortgage, 37, 38, 39, 189
enforcing completion, 51
enforcing covenants, 68, 131 *et seq.*
enquiries, replies to, 20
entry on the register, 102
environmental health officer, 146
essential repairs, 211
estate agent, 15, 46, 129, 202, 223
– in Scotland, 200, 222, 223
– particulars, 18
estimates, 119, 120, 123, 138
eviction, 155, 174
– order, 149, 186
exceptions and reservations, 60
excess service charge, 117
exchange of contracts, 24, 25, 26, 46, gl.
– and deposit, 30
– in person, 26
exclusion clause, 79, 82
exclusion notice, 145, 150
exclusive possession, 11
express co-ownership, 111
express covenants, 84, 140
express terms, 141

factor, 214, 215, 220
fag end of lease, 170, 171
fair wear and tear, 91
family home, 99, 104, 184, 186

Federation of Private Residents' Association, 124
fee, mortgagee's solicitor, 16, 44
fees of managing agents, 125
feu, 198
feuar, 199
feudal tenure, 198
feuduty, 199, 216
feuing conditions, 199
financial contribution, 96, 100, 107, 205
Financial Services Act 1986, 39
first refusal, 180
fit for human habitation, 81, 82, 141, 153, 154
fixed price, Scotland, 200
fixed term lease, 12 *et seq.*
fixtures, 16, 24, 25, 56, 63, gl.
– and stamp duty, 56
flat sharers, 43, 94 *et seq.*
flying freehold, 14
foreclosure, 191, 192, gl.
foreseeable damage, 77
forfeiture, 133, 134, 135, 168, 169, 187, gl.
– clause, 65, 169
– of lease, 73
– proceedings, 170
formal enquiries, 46
formal offer, Scotland, 200
fraud, 105
fraudulent misrepresentation, 48
freehold, 10, 28, 66, gl.
– flat, 13, 14
– flats, and mortgage, 13
– landlord not owning, 13
– landlord retaining, 9
– landlord selling, 7, 68 *et seq.*
– tenants buying, 14, 163, 178 *et seq.*
– what it is, 11
fringe lenders, 42, 43

garage, 18, 116

gazumping, 20, 21
– Scotland, 203, 224
general improvement area, 158
General Register of Sasines, 204, 206
grant aid, 158 *et seq.*
green form scheme, 123, 139
ground flat, Scotland, 209, 213, 215
ground rent, 12, 13, 17, 54, 62, 88, 107, 114, 125, 126, 129, 130, 133, 134, 162, 168, 184, 194, 197, gl.
– low, 56
– non payment of, 133, 134, 135
– withholding, 137, 138
grounds for possession, 173

habendum, 58, 62
harassment, 88, 132, 143, 175, 214
Health and Safety at Work Act 1974, 145
High Court, 83, 164, 189
Housing (Scotland) Act 1987, 218, 220
Housing Act 1985, 8, 153
housing advice centre, 139
Housing Bill 1988, 8, 187
Housing Defects Act 1984, 221

illegal use of premises, 136, 173
immoral purpose, 130, 173
implied
– co-ownership, 112
– covenant, 67, 73, 84, 86
– duty of care, 150
– obligation, 92, 131, 141, 142
– term, 141
– term in mortgage deed, 44
– trust, 104
– trust for sale, 105
improvement, 26, 88, 157
– areas, 153
– grant, 153, 155, 159
– notice, 146
income support scheme, 190
indemnity covenant, 67, 68, 72, 73, 85, 86

injunction, 131, 132, 148
innocent misrepresentation, 49
Insolvency Act 1986, 186
insolvent landlord, 120
inspecting planning register, 20
inspection, personal, 18, 46, 77, 78, 110, 140
insurance, 13, 41, 63, 87, 90, 122, 165, 173, 217, 219, 220
– for gazumping, 21
– for whole block, 41
– policy, 27, 38, 87
interest on mortgage, 38, 42, 43, 112
intermediate grants, 158
interposed management company, 130
intestacy, 94, 95, 205
inventory, 25

joint mortgage, 112
joint tenancy, 94, 95, 96,
– severing, 96
joint tenants, 105, 111, gl.

known hazards, 78, 150

land certificate, 33, gl.
land charges, 47, 112, 179
– register, 29, gl.
– search, 46
Land Register for Scotland, 204, 206
Land Registration Act 1988, 29, 167
Land Registry, 27, 29, 33, 44, 47, 55, 112, gl.
– fees, 15
Landlord and Tenant Act 1954, 169, 172
Landlord and Tenant Act 1985, 114, 124
Landlord and Tenant Act 1987, 8, 85, 114, 120, 123, 161, 177
landlord
– claiming possession, 9 *et seq.*, 126, 173

– remaining liable, 70, 178
– selling freehold, 7, 66, 68 *et seq.*, 122, 167, 183
– suing tenant, 138
– terminating lease, 65
– withholding consent, 88
landlord's obligation, 126, 130, 150
Lands Tribunal for Scotland, 199, 213
Latent Defects Act 1986, 80
law centre, 139
Law Society, 21, 123
Law Society of Scotland, 200
lawful eviction, 172
layman's mistakes, 16, 20
lease getting shorter, 12, 37, 73, 171, 178
lease, implied terms, 8
Leasehold Property (Repairs) Act 1938, 136
Leasehold Reform Act 1967, 175
legal action, 75, 91, 123
legal advice, 139, 213
legal aid, 83, 147, 148, 197, 213
legal costs, 83
legal expenses, 106, 213, 223
legal fiction, 97, 98
let the buyer beware, 82
liability
– for injury, 70 *et seq.*, 76 *et seq.*
– for repairs, 201, 208
licensed conveyancer, 15, 46, 75
life assurance, 38
limited company, 126
local authority, 19, 20, 146, 147, 148, 153, 154, 156, 157, 193, 195, 196, 210, 211, 214, 221
– discretion, 158
– repairs, 218
local land charges, 19
local search, 19, gl.

magistrates' court, 147
maintenance, 13, 26, 85, 125, 151, 165, 213
– charges, 201

making an offer Scotland, 202, 203
management, 125
– charge, 12
– company, 121, 145, 151, 161, 182
– company, tenants', 126, 128, 129
manager order, 161 *et seq.*
managing agent, 125, 128
– fees, 116
mandatory grant, 155, 159, 160
marital breakdown, 96, 100
market value of premises, 52, 62, 164
matrimonial home, 100 *et seq.*, 206
Matrimonial Homes Act 1983, 101
Matrimonial Homes (Family Protection) (Scotland) Act 1981, 206
memorandum, 127
merger, 169, 170
– and surrender, 169
middle flat, 215
– owner, 209
minute of waiver, 212
MIRAS, 43, 112
misdescription, 50
misrepresentation, 30, 50, 52
missives, 203, 204, 222, 224, 225
monthly payments, 38
mortgage, 12, 35 *et seq.*, gl.
– application, 196
– arranging, 35 *et seq.*, 202
– arrears, 184, 188 *et seq.*
– certificate, 36
– conditions, 41 *et seq.*
– cost of, 36
– deed, 40, 42, 47, 204, gl.
– default, 36, 44, 184, 187 *et seq.*
– paying off, 30, 34, 40, 41, 42, 225
– repayment, 40 106, 189
– term extending, 184, 189
– term of, 35, 38, 44
mortgagee, 35, 53, gl.
– choice of, 36
– obtaining possession, 188, 189
mortgagor, 35 *et seq.*, 42, gl.

244   *index*

name/address of landlord, 166
negligence, 8, 75, 76 *et seq.*, 141, 143, 150, 217, gl.
negligent advice, 80, 81
negligent misrepresentation, 49
negligent statements, 80
neighbouring property, 20, 140
neighbours, 148, 149, 201, 211, 213, 214, 216, 219
– and noise, 148
new freeholders name of, 68
noise, 93, 144, 148
non-disclosed co-owner, 110, 11.
non-institutional credit companies, 43
non-owning spouse, 100, 101, 207
notice of recognition, 124
notice to complete, 50, 51, 52
notice to quit, 11, 134
nuisance, 8, 89, 141, 144, 146, 147, 152, 173
– order, 147

obligations continuing, 70 *et seq.*
Occupiers Liability Act 1957, 150, 152
options, 58, 177
– to buy, 66, 178, 180
– to renew, 177, 180
oral agreement, 15
original landlord remaining liable, 73, 76
original tenant, 72, 76
– and breach of covenant, 73
other flat owners Scotland, 211, 220
other tenants, 61, 85, 146, 165
outstanding bills, 118
overriding interest, 110, 180, gl.
owning spouse, 100, 206

parliament, 7, 140, 141
past-performance, 22
peaceful enjoyment, 64, 87
pension mortgage, 39

permissive waste, 93
personal injury, 79, 150 *et seq.*
personal search, 20
pets 90, 201, 212
planning permission, 27
positive covenants, 84
possession order, 155, 172, 173, 174, 186, 189, 191
– postponing, 189
power to postpone sale, 98, 99
pre-emption, 177, 179, 180
preliminary enquiries, 17, 18, 140, gl.
– replies to, 50, 77
previous owner, 151, 217
private pension schemes, 39
privity of contract, 75
proceeds of sale, 97, 98, 104, 110
– clearing mortgage debt, 191
professional, 75 *et seq.*, 80
– avoiding liability, 81
– fees, 15
– indemnity, 16
– liability, 77
– mistake, 16, 75 *et seq.*
profit rental, 130
prohibitions, 212
property adjustment order, 103
property centre, 222
prospective buyer, 140, 183, 223
Protection from Eviction Act 1977, 175, 177
provisos, 58
– and options, 65
Public Health Act 1936, 147
purchase price, 16, 24, 25
– contributing to, 100, 103, 104, 105, 106, 109
– extra to, 25

qualifying tenants, 181
quiet enjoyment, 64, 87, 92, 142

ready-made company, 126
'reasonable person', 77, 83, 91, 143

receivership, 191
recognised tenants' association, 119, 129
reddendum, 58, 62
redemption fee, 41
Register House in Edinburgh, 208
registered, 46, 110
– protection, 112
– system, 27
– title, 29, gl.
registration, 101, 178
– protecting rights, 29
Rent Act 1977, 172
– protection, 45, 172
rent, 92
– action, 133
– arrears, 137
– payment of, 107
rent assessment committee, 123, 124, 164
rental purchase, 45
repair, 13, 63, 85, 86, 125, 151, 165
– and maintenance, 16
– covenant, 72, 140, 145, 155
– covenant, breach of, 77
– notice, 154, 156, 218
repairs, 26, 90 *et seq.*, 213
– grant, 159, 217
– obligation, 59, 87
repayment mortgage, 38, 40, 106, 189
requisitions, 29, 30
– replies to, 77
rescission, 48
reserve fund, 115
residents' association, 119, 129, 214
resulting trust, 105 *et seq.*, 112
right of first refusal, 180
right of pre-emption, 66
right to buy, 184, 193, 196, 197
– and clawback, 195
– and discount, 195, 196
– and mortgage, 195, 196, 197
– and registration, 197

– mortgages, 44
right to information, 166
roof, in Scotland, 209, 211, 213, 216

safety, 149
schedule, 57, 58, 60, 67, 115
Scotland, 198 *et seq.*
secure tenant, 193, 194, gl.
security, 204
– for mortgage, 35, 37, 38, 43, 53, 191
security of tenure, 169, 173, gl.
seller's mortgage, 33, 34
selling flat in Scotland, 222 *et seq.*
separate price, 25
service charge, 12, 16, 17, 64, 86, 88, 114 *et seq.*, 122, 125, 126, 129, 130, 162, 165, 166
– calculation of, 88
– time of payment, 117
services provided, 85, 125
severance of joint tenancy, 96
shared ownership lease, 196, 197
sinking fund, 17, 115, 116, 121, 122
sitting tenant, 52, 53
slum clearance, 153, 157
solicitors, 15, 75, 81, 113, 116, 148, 170
– in Scotland, 199 *et seq.*, 222 *et seq.*
– property centres, 199
– monopoly, 15
special conditions, 23
special grant, 160
specific performance, 51, 131, 132, 133
specific prohibitions, 90
specimen lease, 57 *et seq.*
spouse, 100, 186, 223
stakeholder, 31, 32
stamp duty, 15, 47, 55, 56, 204, gl.
– exemption from, 55
standard form of contract, 22, 49, 51, 52
standard security, 204
statutory charge, 139

statutory nuisance, 147
statutory tenant, 173
straight loan, 112
structural alterations, 41
structural survey, 19, 202
subject to contract, 15, 20, 21
subletting, 7, 10, 67, 72, 137
– landlord's consent to, 88
substantial repairs, 156
subtenants, 7, 10, 67, 72, 170, gl.
– breaches by, 72
suing for deposit, 32
superior, 198, 212
supplementary benefit, 190
surrender, 170
survey, 18, 46, 140, 202
– fees, 52
– type of, 78, 202
surveyor, 75, 122, 129, 219, 224
survivorship destination, 206

tax relief, 39, 43, 112
tenancy in common, 94, 95, 96
tenant buying freehold, 68, 126,
  128, 129, 169, 177
tenant remaining in possession,
  173 *et seq.*
tenant suing landlord, 144
tenant's liability, 120, 152
tenants in common, 97, 105, 111,
  gl.
tenants' association, 119, 122, 123
– recognised, 123 *et seq.*
– and estimates, 123
Tenants' Rights etc. (Scotland) Act
  1980, 220
third parties, 100, 137
– causing damage, 143
– rights, 27, 29, 44, 47, 101, 102
– undisclosed, 18, 29
time and place notice, 155
time limits, 79
– and contract, 75, 79
– and negligence, 78, 79, 80
– and personal injury, 79, 80

– for court action, 75, 80, 82, 133
time of the essence, 50, 52, gl.
top flat owner, 209
trust, 26
– for sale, 97, 98, 99, 104, 106
– for sale, implied, 104 *et seq.*
trust fund, 120
– distribution of, 121
– holding in, 26
– service charges, 120
trustee for sale buying from, 98
trustee, 98, gl.
– in bankruptcy, 185
types of survey, 78, 202

underlease, 10, 54, 66, 67, 169
unfit for human habitation, 153
  et seq., 157
unfit housing, 141, 157
unlawful eviction, 175
upset price, 200
urgent repairs, 217
usual covenants, 84, 92

vacant possession, 23, 30, 50, 111,
  164, 174, 190, 194
valuation, 18, 194, 202
– fee, 19
– fee saving on, 19
– report, 19
value of the property, 37
– increasing, 27, 35
variable service charges, 124
variation of lease, 161, 164 *et seq.*
visitors, 143, 150, 151
voluntary waste, 93
voting rights, 127

warrant of execution, 133
waste, 135
will, 94, 95, 96, 205, 206
withdrawing from contract, 21,
  29, 30, 48, 49

yielding and paying, 57, 58

some other Consumer Publications

What to do after an accident £6.95

explains your legal rights when another person's negligence has caused you harm and how to set about claiming compensation. It deals with accidents on the road (as driver, passenger, pedestrian, cyclist), at home (your own or someone else's), at work, when out and about. The book provides guidance on court proceedings, negotiating through lawyers, assessing damages, making insurance claims, applying for statutory payments. There is also advice on medical treatment and coping with disability and getting back to work, with the names of organisations providing help and support.

Taking your own case to court or tribunal £3.95

is for people who do not have a solicitor to represent them in a county court or magistrates' court or before a tribunal. This book tells you the procedures to follow in preparing and presenting your case, what happens at the hearing, what steps can be taken to enforce a judgment, how to appeal if the judgment goes against you. It explains in layman's terms how to conduct proceedings yourself in the county court (arbitration for 'small claims' and open court hearings), in the High Court (rarely appropriate for a litigant-in-person), in a magistrates' court (for both civil and criminal matters), at a social security appeal tribunal (challenging a DHSS benefits decision) and before an industrial tribunal (dismissal cases). There is a chapter dealing with possession cases.

Making the most of higher education £6.95

is a practical guide for both the 18+ student and the mature student, giving advice about choosing subjects and courses (with an eye to career prospects), getting a place at a university, polytechnic or other college, applications and interviews. It also advises on ways of studying effectively towards a degree, making ends meet on a grant, planning for a career, and many other student problems.

Which? way to buy, sell and move house £9.95

Whatever you are moving from or to, this book is an invaluable guide to what is involved.

It clarifies issues that have to be decided initially, such as location (town v country), type of property (house v flat), size and style. The expenses likely to arise are set out, from statutory fees to thank-you presents for helpers, with basic information about getting a mortgage.

There is advice on 'house-hunting' generally, with a detailed section on what to look out for when viewing a flat – discussing the advantages and disadvantages of which floor, layout, heating, outgoings, garaging.

The book goes carefully through the procedure of making an offer, having a valuation and/or survey (including of a flat), conveyancing, exchange of contracts, completion. Problem areas are pointed out: the 'chain' of buyers and sellers, bridging loans, insurance, fixtures and fittings (to buy or not to buy).

Many practical matters have to be dealt with between contract and completion and there is a comprehensive section on what has to be done at this interim stage (eg getting gas/electricity, telephone services organised), including a helpful checklist for change of address notifications.

Once the date of the move has been fixed, the arrangements for the actual removal can be made – by a professional firm or by doing it yourself with a hired van. The various factors to consider with either method are discussed, such as cost, insurance, personal wear and tear. A timetable for the moving operation guides you to what will need to be done at different stages, and there are useful hints on the practicalities of packing, disposing of unwanted possessions, organising the household (pets to kennels, children to friends). Activities on the traumatic day of the move are itemised, and what will still have to be done afterwards.

As a mirror image, the process of selling your property is also dealt with. And there are sections on buying and selling in Scotland.

As well as a wealth of factual information, the book is enlivened by direct quotes from people who have recently gone through the process of moving, with comments and hints based on their experiences.

Earning money at home £6.95

explains how to brush up a skill or hobby into a money-making venture. It gives advice on organising your family and domestic life, on advertising your activities, costing and selling your work, dealing with customers. There is information on statutory and financial requirements for insurance, tax, accounts, VAT, employing others. The book suggests ways in which your experience from a previous job could be utilised, or a skill or hobby developed to a professional standard, or how unexploited energy and ability can be used profitably. Suggestions are made for improving your skills to a higher standard, and the names and addresses are given of organisations that might be helpful.

Starting your own business   £6.95

It's in at the deep end for many people who want to set up
their own business. It represents a challenge and an adventure, but needs hard information on finance, marketing,
tax, insurance, premises, employing others and, above all,
how to choose the right business project.

Starting your own business explains the steps to be taken for
the getting and the spending of business money, from
applying for a government grant and taking advantage
of agencies that offer funds and advice, to cash flow
forecasting, pricing policy, keeping business records and
preparing a balance sheet. It discusses the different ways of
trading, the pros and cons of franchises or buying an
existing business, and explains the law for consumers –
from the other side of the counter.

This book was first published in 1983 – since then,
everyone in Britain has become aware of the part that small
businesses have to play in the economy. Whatever business
the reader is thinking of starting, there is a lot to be learned
and a lot of information to be gathered.

Understanding stress   £6.95

Stress is inherent in the human condition and our century
has intensified many stresses and added new ones, many of
them psychological or social in nature. Some stresses are
related to, or follow on, a specific identifiable event in the
person's life: death, divorce, imprisonment rank high on
the list. This book deals with stress and life events, stress
from the world around us, at work, in the family. It explains
the bodily reactions to stress and how to recognise the
warning signs and how to help oneself cope with stress.

Understanding back trouble £6.95

will help the countless suffers from back trouble to understand what has happened to them and why. The structure of the spine is explained and illustrated, with a comprehensive account of possible malfunctions. Readers are told how to cope with a sudden attack of back pain and what treatments, both orthodox and 'alternative' are currently available. There is also advice for sufferers of long standing.

Prevention is all-important. For those with healthy backs who want to keep them so, this book tells how to go about daily work and leisure so as to minimise the risk of back strain. A range of exercises for back sufferers is described in detail.

Wills and probate £6.95

There are still too many people who have not made their will. This book will help them to do so, not blindly but aware of all the tax implications, the consequences of divorce, the right choice of executors, the proper signing and witnessing of the will so that their wishes can be carried out simply and sensibly.

The second part of the book describes what has to be done, administratively, by the executors of the estate of someone who has died. The probate registry provides special machinery to deal with laymen who wish to do so without having a solicitor. This book supplements this by explaining, in detail, not only the probate registry procedure but all that goes before and what comes after. It highlights recent relevant changes in tax law and procedure.

The book explains the law and procedure in England and Wales and briefly explains the main differences which apply in Scotland.

What to do when someone dies £6.95

is a companion volume to *Wills and probate*. It aims to help those who have never had to deal with the arrangements that must be made after a death – getting a doctor's certificate and registering the death, deciding whether to bury or cremate, choosing an undertaker and a coffin, putting notices in the papers, selecting the form of service, claiming national insurance benefits. It explains the function of people with whom they will come in contact, often for the first time. They will get help and guidance from the doctor, the registrar, the undertaker, the clergyman, the cemetery or crematorium officials, the Department of Health and Social Security and, in some circumstances, the police and the coroner. However, it is the executor or nearest relative who has to make the decisions, often at a time of personal distress. The book describes what needs to be done, when, and how to set about it.

No attempt is made to deal with the personal or social aspects of death, such as the psychology of grief and shock, the rituals and conventions of mourning, or attitudes to death.

Divorce – legal procedures and financial facts
£6.95

explains the special procedure for an undefended divorce and deals with the financial facts to be faced when a marriage ends in divorce. Aspects covered include getting legal advice, conciliation, legal aid and its drawbacks, the various financial and property orders the court can make, what can happen to the matrimonial home, the children, how to calculate needs and resources, the effect of tax, coping with shortage of money after divorce.

Understanding cancer £6.95

explains the nature and causes of the disease most people
find more frightening than any other. It tells you how to
recognise some of the symptoms and avoid some of the
risks, and explains how cancer is diagnosed. It goes into the
details of various forms of treatment: surgery, radiotherapy,
chemotherapy, including their possible side effects, and
takes an objective look at the role of alternative/complemen-
tary therapies. It describes some of the advances in cancer
research but does not pretend that these will soon provide
the long awaited cure. The book deals with advanced cancer
and terminal care but stresses that cancer must not be
regarded as inevitably fatal.

Consumer Publications are available from Consumers'
Association, Castlemead, Gascoyne Way, Hertford
SG14 1LH, and from booksellers.